The Neuroleptic-Nonresponsive Patient: Characterization and Treatment

Compliments of

David Spiegel, M.D.
Series Editor

The Neuroleptic-Nonresponsive Patient: Characterization and Treatment

Edited by
Burt Angrist, M.D.
S. Charles Schulz, M.D.

American Psychiatric Press, Inc.

Washington, DC
London, England

Copyright © 1990 American Psychiatric Press, Inc.
ALL RIGHTS RESERVED
Manufactured in the United States of America
First Edition   93 92 91 90   4 3 2

American Psychiatric Press, Inc., 1400 K Street, N.W.
Washington, DC 20005.

The paper used in this publication meets the minimum requirements of the American National Standard for Information Sciences — Permanence of Paper for Printed Library Materials, ANSI Z39.48-1984.   ∞

Library of Congress Cataloging-in-Publication Data

The Neuroleptic nonresponsive patient: characterization and treatment/edited by Burt Angrist, S. Charles Schulz. — 1st ed.
     p. cm. — (Progress in psychiatry; no. 27)
    Contains updated articles originally presented at the 1988 American Psychiatric Association Meeting.
    Includes bibliographical references.
    ISBN 0-88048-461-6 (alk. paper)
    1. Schizophrenia—Chemotherapy—Congresses. 2. Antipsychotic drugs—Congresses. I. Angrist, B. II. Schulz, S. Charles. III. American Psychiatric Association. Meeting (141st: 1988: Montreal, Quebec) IV. Series
    [DNLM: 1. Schizophrenia—drug therapy—congresses. 2. Tranquilizing Agents, Major—therapeutic use—congresses. WM 203 N4933]
RC514.N444   1990
616.89'82061—dc20
DNLM/DLC
for Library of Congress   90-235
                                                       CIP

British Cataloguing in Publication Data

A CIP record is available from the British Library.

Contents

Refinements of
Neuroleptic Treatment

Treatment for
Neuroleptic-Refractory Patients

Contributors

Burt Angrist, M.D.
Professor of Psychiatry, New York University School of Medicine, and Staff Psychiatrist, New York Veterans Administration Medical Center, New York, New York

Robert W. Baker, M.D.
Director of Special Studies Center, University of Pittsburgh and Mayview State Hospital, and Assistant Professor of Psychiatry, University of Pittsburgh, Pittsburgh, Pennsylvania

Jeffrey L. Berlant, M.D., Ph.D.
Director of Outpatient Services, Fair Oaks Hospital, Summit, New Jersey

Malcolm B. Bowers, Jr., M.D.
Professor of Psychiatry, Yale University School of Medicine, New Haven, Connecticut

Robert R. Conley, M.D.
Research Assistant Professor, University of Maryland, Maryland Psychiatric Research Center, and Director, Treatment Resistant Unit, Spring Grove Hospital Center, Baltimore, Maryland

Michael Davidson, M.D.
Department of Psychiatry and Schizophrenia Biological Research Center, Bronx Veterans Administration Medical Center, Department of Psychiatry and Pharmacology, Mount Sinai School of Medicine, New York, New York

Kenneth L. Davis, M.D.
Department of Psychiatry and Schizophrenia Biological Research Center, Bronx Veterans Administration Medical Center, Department of Psychiatry and Pharmacology, Mount Sinai School of Medicine, New York, New York

Thomas B. Horvath, M.D.
Professor of Psychiatry, Mount Sinai School of Medicine, and Professor of Psychiatry, State University of New York Health Science Center at Brooklyn, and Chief of Staff, Brooklyn Veterans Administration Medical Center, Brooklyn, New York

Celeste A. Johns, M.D.
Department of Psychiatry, The Mary Imogene Bassett Hospital, Cooperstown, New York

E. Michael Kahn, M.D.
Medical Director, Nashua Mental Health Inpatient Unit, Northeast
Psychiatric Associates, and Brookside Hospital, Nashua, New
Hampshire

John M. Kane, M.D.
Chairman, Department of Psychiatry, Hillside Hospital, Division of
Long Island Jewish Medical Center, Glen Oaks, New York

Richard S. E. Keefe, M.A.
Department of Psychiatry and Schizophrenia Biological Research
Center, Bronx Veterans Administration Medical Center, Department
of Psychiatry and Pharmacology, Mount Sinai School of Medicine,
New York, New York

Jeffrey A. Lieberman, M.D.
Director of Research, Hillside Hospital, Division of Long Island
Jewish Medical Center, Glen Oaks, New York

Miklos F. Losonczy, Ph.D., M.D.
Department of Psychiatry and Schizophrenia Biological Research
Center, Bronx Veterans Administration Medical Center, Department
of Psychiatry and Pharmacology, Mount Sinai School of Medicine,
New York, New York

Stephen R. Marder, M.D.
Associate Professor of Psychiatry, Veterans Administration Medical
Center, Brentwood Division, Los Angeles, California

David I. Mayerhoff, M.D.
Department of Research, Hillside Hospital, Division of Long Island
Jewish Medical Center, Glen Oaks, New York

Kamal K. Midha, Ph.D., D.Sc.
Professor of Pharmacology, University of Saskatchewan, Saskatoon,
Saskatchewan, Canada

Richard C. Mohs, Ph.D.
Department of Psychiatry and Schizophrenia Biological Research
Center, Bronx Veterans Administration Medical Center, Department
of Psychiatry and Pharmacology, Mount Sinai School of Medicine,
New York, New York

David Pickar, M.D.
Acting Chief, Clinical Neuroscience Branch, National Institute of
Mental Health, Rockville, Maryland

Mark H. Rapaport, M.D.
Schizophrenia Research Branch, National Institute of Mental Health,
Rockville, Maryland

S. Charles Schulz, M.D.
Professor and Chairman, Case Western Reserve University, Department of Psychiatry, Cleveland, Ohio

Jeremy M. Silverman, Ph.D.
Department of Psychiatry and Schizophrenia Biological Research Center, Bronx Veterans Administration Medical Center, Department of Psychiatry and Pharmacology, Mount Sinai School of Medicine, New York, New York

Theodore Van Putten, M.D.
Adjunct Professor of Psychiatry, Veterans Administration Medical Center, Brentwood Division, Los Angeles, California

William Wirshing, M.D.
Assistant Professor of Psychiatry, Veterans Administration Medical Center, Brentwood Division, Los Angeles, California

Adam Wolkin, M.D.
Assistant Professor, New York University School of Medicine, New York University Veterans Administration Medical Center, New York, New York

Owen M. Wolkowitz, M.D.
Assistant Professor of Psychiatry, and Director, Behavioral Neuroscience Service, Langley Porter Psychiatric Institute, University of California, San Francisco Medical Center, San Francisco, California

Introduction to the
Progress in Psychiatry *Series*

The *Progress in Psychiatry* Series is designed to capture in print the excitement that comes from assembling a diverse group of experts from various locations to examine in detail the newest information about a developing aspect of psychiatry. This series emerged as a collaboration between the American Psychiatric Association's (APA) Scientific Program Committee and the American Psychiatric Press, Inc. Great interest is generated by a number of the symposia presented each year at the APA Annual Meeting, and we realized that much of the information presented there, carefully assembled by people who are deeply immersed in a given area, would unfortunately not appear together in print. The symposia sessions at the annual meetings provide an unusual opportunity for experts who otherwise might not meet on the same platform to share their diverse viewpoints for a period of 3 hours. Some new themes are repeatedly reinforced and gain credence, while in other instances disagreements emerge, enabling the audience and now the reader to reach informed decisions about new directions in the field. The *Progress in Psychiatry* Series allows us to publish and capture some of the best of the symposia and thus provide an in-depth treatment of specific areas that might not otherwise be presented in broader review formats.

Psychiatry is by nature an interface discipline, combining the study of mind and brain, of individual and social environments, of the humane and the scientific. Therefore, progress in the field is rarely linear—it often comes from unexpected sources. Further, new developments emerge from an array of viewpoints that do not necessarily provide immediate agreement but rather expert examination of the issues. We intend to present innovative ideas and data that will enable you, the reader, to participate in this process.

We believe the *Progress in Psychiatry* Series will provide you with an opportunity to review timely new information in specific fields of interest as they are developing. We hope you find that the excitement of the presentations is captured in the written word and that this book proves to be informative and enjoyable reading.

David Spiegel, M.D.
Series Editor
Progress in Psychiatry Series

Progress in Psychiatry Series Titles

Introduction

Psychotic patients who prove unresponsive or inadequately responsive to neuroleptics often remain significantly impaired after standard treatment and require extended institutional support. However, such support is currently in such short supply that it is often, realistically, unavailable—as is evident from the large numbers of homeless psychiatric patients now living in our cities.

The purpose of this volume is to assist clinicians who treat such neuroleptic-refractory patients. We also hope that clinical researchers in this area will find the volume useful for its comments on methodology, literature review, theoretical concepts proposed, and new data presented.

GENERAL CONSIDERATIONS

The precise number of patients poorly responsive to neuroleptics is not easy to determine. The number certainly varies from hospital to hospital since these patients tend to "migrate" to chronic care facilities.

Davis et al. (1980) reviewed the large, now classic body of data generated by the National Institute of Mental Health Psychopharmacology Research Branch in their multicenter studies in the 1960s (Cole et al. 1964, 1966; Goldberg et al. 1965). The data showed that in controlled studies of newly admitted patients who received active treatment, a little less than 10% were rated "no change" or "worse" and somewhat more than 20% were considered only "minimally improved" (Davis et al. 1980, p. 71). Kane et al. (1988) indicated that these data justified a conservative estimate that 10–20% of patients "derive little benefit from typical neuroleptic drug therapy" (p. 789).

The findings noted above of just less than 10% of newly admitted schizophrenic patients being rated unchanged or worse is also consistent with the findings for short-term outcome in the Northwick Park Study of First Episodes of Schizophrenia, in which 17 of 263 (6.5%) such patients were unable to be discharged within the time of the study (MacMillan et al. 1986). However, newly admitted and particularly first-break patients may be more responsive to neuroleptics than the schizophrenic population as a whole. Studies in these populations may thus underestimate the problem of neuroleptic nonresponse.

Kolakowska et al. (1985) did an intensive cross-sectional study of 77 patients with schizophrenia of 2–20 years' duration. Of these 77, 20 (26%) had a "*poor outcome* (i.e., chronic psychotic or defect state): persistent hallucinations and/or delusions which affect behavior together with moderate or severe negative symptoms: social isolation, poor self care" (p. 231). In general, these patients were characterized by earlier age of onset of illness and more prominent negative symptoms during the first episode. Their neuroleptic response was usually poor, even in early episodes of illness. These findings suggest that this poor outcome was related to a more severe subtype of illness rather than to stage of illness, however, some loss of neuroleptic responsiveness over time was also noted. Of the 25 who had proven neuroleptic refractory in their *last* hospitalization, 14 had never responded to neuroleptics; 11 had shown at least partial responses in their first one to four hospitalizations.

Another interesting source of information about rate of response/nonresponse in unselected patients is the very early group of papers on antipsychotic drug use in hospitals for the first time. In this situation, a cross section of acute and chronic patients had their first exposure to these agents, thereby ensuring a natural "mix" of potential responders and nonresponders. In this unique "natural experiment," a (cursory) literature review is summarized in Table I-1. In these 10 early studies the percentage of patients failing to show major clinical improvement ranged from just over 17% (Denber and Bird 1957) to 51% (Barsa and Kline 1955) with a mean of 32%. Some caveats to these data that must be emphasized are that the studies were not "blind" and effects of antipsychotic agents were so striking at the time that investigators soon became very enthusiastic indeed (J. Barsa, personal communication 1984). It must also be remembered that the diagnostic criteria for schizophrenia were extremely broad at that time.

In 6 of these 10 studies it was specifically noted that chronic patients showed less brisk therapeutic responses than acute/recently hospitalized patients. This finding may indicate loss of neuroleptic responsiveness over time but an alternate interpretation could be that delay in treatment itself may predispose to a worse outcome. Two modern studies echo this theme. The Northwick Park study (Crow et al. 1986) found that duration between onset of symptoms and treatment was

Table I-1. Percentage of schizophrenic patients failing to show major clinical improvement after initial treatment with chlorpromazine in early trials

Author(s)	Percentage	Specific notation of decreased therapeutic effect in chronic patients	Comments
Lehman and Hanrahan 1954	33	Yes	—
Bird et al. 1955	23	Yes	Mixed diagnoses 76% "Dementia Praecox"
Barsa and Kline 1955	51(41.5% slightly improved; 9.3% unimproved)	Yes	Used chlorpromazine and reserpine combined
Kinross-Wright 1955	28(14% slight improvement, 14% unchanged)	—	—
Szatmari 1956	33(chronic patients) 40(acute patients)	No	
Ayd 1956	28	Yes	—
Brooks 1956	30(1.8% unchanged 28% "quiet, tractable and cooperative")	Yes	Used chlorpromazine and reserpine combined
Pachter 1957	29	Most patients chronic	—
Winkelman 1957	39(17% slight improvement; 22% unchanged)	Yes	—
Denber and Bird 1957	17	—	Mixed diagnoses 68% "Dementia Praecox"
Mean	32		

a strong predictor of relapse liability. The classic studies of May et al. (1976) comparing psychotherapy, drug treatment, and combined therapy suggested a worse outcome after discharge for patients initially assigned to psychotherapy. Thus the possibility that delay in treatment may itself be deleterious for long-term outcome cannot be dismissed lightly.

CRITERIA FOR NONRESPONSE

The prevalence of neuroleptic nonresponse will vary, of course, with the criteria used for its definition. A very rigorous set of research criteria proposed for use in the multicenter trial of clozapine (Kane et al. 1988) was as follows: 1) historical—no period of good functioning within the preceding 5 years with neuroleptics (from at least two chemical classes) at doses equal to or greater than 1,000 mg/day of chlorpromazine for 6 weeks without "significant symptomatic relief"; 2) cross-sectional—Brief Psychiatric Rating Scale (BPRS) (Overall and Gorham 1962) score of at least 45 (standard 18-item version in which 1 = absent and 7 = very severe), Clinical Global Impression (CGI) (Guy 1976) score of at least 4 (moderately ill), and item scores of at least 4 ("moderate") for two of the following four items: conceptual disorganization, suspiciousness, hallucinatory behavior, and unusual thought content; 3) prospective—failure to decrease BPRS score by 20% or below 35, or failure to decrease CGI score to 3 ("mildly ill") after a 6-week prospective trial of haloperidol up to 60 mg/day.

In practice, even these rigorous and very explicit criteria can be difficult to apply. For example, some patients who easily meet historical and cross-sectional criteria may worsen when present neuroleptics are discontinued and may increase their BPRS score dramatically. Reinstitution of treatment at this "new baseline" leads to a greater than 20% reduction in psychopathology score. Thus, in retrospect, such patients would be considered (despite their unacceptable status with treatment) to be at least partially responsive. Such patients should probably be classified as inadequate responders rather than "treatment refractory." Nonetheless, we believe such patients should be considered eligible for the treatment strategies discussed in this volume.

Common sense dictates that the criteria the clinician uses in choosing patients for neuroleptic augmentation strategies be somewhat flexible and related to the risk of the approach to be used. For relatively innocuous strategies such as dose change, plasma level titration, or short-term addition of low-dose benzodiazepines, dissatisfaction with the patient's psychiatric status after 6–12 weeks of standard neuroleptic therapy and a sense that he or she "could do better" may well be perfectly proper. For the use of agents with a greater risk potential (such as carbamazepine or certainly clozapine), more rigorous documentation of chronic impairments is suggested; that is, the guidelines above should be roughly followed.

CONTENTS

In recognition of the problems in treating neuroleptic-refractory (or poorly responsive) patients, the editors organized a symposium at the 1988 American Psychiatric Association meeting. This symposium focused on a variety of clinical trials of strategies for treating such patients. Dr. Johns indicated that additional time at the same neuroleptic dose often produced the same results as increased dose. Dr. Wolkowitz reviewed his studies of alprazolam augmentation and discussed discrete, briskly responsive and nonresponsive patient subgroups and the differing changes in plasma homovanillic acid (HVA) that responsive and nonresponsive patients showed (Wolkowitz et al. 1988). Dr. Schulz discussed his own and others' (generally favorable) data on the use of adjunctive lithium and the somewhat more limited body of his own and others' data on the effect of combined treatment with neuroleptics and carbamazepine. Dr. Berlant noted striking improvement in up to 50% of patients who had a poor response to neuroleptics after combined treatment with reserpine. Finally, Dr. Kane reviewed the results of the rigorous multicenter trial of clozapine versus chlorpromazine/benztropine, which showed superior efficacy for clozapine so convincingly (Kane et al. 1988). These presentations have been updated for this volume.

The order of the presentations was chosen intentionally to represent a continuum of the most conservative to boldest options that clinicians have at their disposal. For this volume we also solicited some more basic chapters that might give insight into mechanisms underlying neuroleptic response versus nonresponse (or at least current thinking on this subject). This more basic section supports the concept that dopamine receptor blockade initiates secondary events, which decrease presynaptic activity, and that this decrease contributes to antipsychotic effects. It is reasonable to hypothesize that such secondary effects fail to develop in neuroleptic nonresponders.

There are several lines of evidence that support this concept. First is the discrepancy between the time required for receptor blockade and antipsychotic effects. Dopamine receptor occupancy can be demonstrated by competition for labeled receptor legends in the striata of animals pretreated only hours before assay. That this occupancy has behavioral relevance is shown by the fact that as little as

1 hour pretreatment can block the effects of dopaminergic agonist drugs such as amphetamine or apomorphine. In contrast, antipsychotic effects generally evolve over a period of some weeks (for full effect); initial affectual indifference to symptoms, as frequently expressed by patients in the words "those voices (or ideas) are still there but they don't bother me as much," can often be seen more acutely. Second are the studies of plasma HVA. Preclinical studies showed that plasma and brain HVA changed in parallel after drugs affecting dopaminergic function in both rodents (Bacopoulos et al. 1979; Kendler et al. 1981, 1982) and subhuman primates (Bacopoulos et al. 1978, 1980). These studies suggested that plasma HVA might reflect central dopaminergic turnover. Subsequently it was shown that plasma HVA levels correlated with ratings of severity of illness in schizophrenic patients (Davis et al. 1985). Finally, and most directly implicating presynaptic regulation in antipsychotic efficacy, was the demonstration by Pickar et al. (1984, 1986) that, with neuroleptic treatment, decrements in plasma HVA correlated in time with decreases in symptomatology. Conversely, after neuroleptic discontinuation, the plasma HVA increased in close temporal relationship with symptom exacerbation.

One electrophysiologic effect of chronic neuroleptics that both has a similar time course to evolve as antipsychotic effects and that reduces presynaptic activity and dopamine turnover is depolarization blockade (Bunney et al. 1987, and references therein). Thus depolarization blockade is currently believed by many researchers to be a candidate for the "missing" step(s) between initial receptor blockade and later-evolving antipsychotic effects.

The chapters in the section entitled "Clinical and Biological Studies of Poorly Responsive Patients" further support the concept that neuroleptic nonresponders fail to develop the secondary consequences (depolarization arrest) of chronic receptor blockade. Bowers (Chapter 2) demonstrates that rapid neuroleptic responders show a plasma HVA pattern of initial elevation and rapid decline with treatment, whereas less briskly responsive patients tend to show low initial plasma HVA levels that change much less (if at all) with treatment. This finding is consistent with previously expressed concepts of plasticity and autoregulation of central dopamine systems (Davila 1989; Friedhoff 1986) and with Bowers' (1984) earlier findings of persistently elevated cerebrospinal fluid HVA in neuroleptic nonresponsive patients.

Wolkin (Chapter 3) describes a positron emission tomography study using the dopamine receptor legend *N*-methylspiroperidol that shows that very rigorously defined responders and nonresponders have equal occupancy of dopamine receptors by haloperidol after treatment (thus demonstrating nonresponse not to be a function of increased hepatic metabolism or blood-brain barrier impenetrability). Additionally, Wolkin shows an orderly but not linear increase of dopamine receptor blockade with increasing plasma haloperidol levels, thus providing rational guidelines for relating plasma levels of this agent with receptor occupancy. This work also provides a rational basis for the uniformly negative results of studies using rapid "digitalization" doses of neuroleptics (Donlon et al. 1978; Ericksen et al. 1978) or "megadose" therapy (Goldberg et al. 1972; Hollister and Kim 1982; Quitkin et al. 1975).

FUTURE DIRECTIONS

The focus of this volume is the active work ongoing with respect to demographics, clinical trials, studies of mechanisms, and new treatment approaches. It seems appropriate to indicate here some of these relevant studies in progress.

Regarding prevalence of neuroleptic nonresponse and its relationship to the longitudinal course of schizophrenia, data can be anticipated from two long-term longitudinal studies in progress of first-break schizophrenic patients (Lieberman et al., Hillside/Long Island Jewish Medical Center and Albert Einstein College of Medicine; and DeLisi et al., Central Islip Psychiatric Center and SUNY Stony Brook). Regarding clinical response data, the relationship between clinical effects and neuroleptic plasma levels are discussed by Van Putten et al. (Chapter 5, this volume) and are further being explored via "titration" of the same patients into a variety of plasma level ranges in a study in progress by Volovka et al. (Manhattan and Rockland Psychiatric Centers, New York University).

Benzodiazepine augmentation of neuroleptic response is an area of active study. Douyon et al. (1989) have shown a relationship between high alprazolam levels and good clinical response. This may lead some clinicians to use high-dose alprazolam for unresponsive patients. To do so involves *significant* dangers since alprazolam withdrawal can be precipitous, severe, and potentially fatal. In addition, a large study by Csernansky et al. (1988) has shown apparent tolerance to the initial beneficial effects of alprazolam.

Lorazepam has been reported to be an effective adjunct to neuroleptics for acute behavioral control, so much so that only half the dose of neuroleptic is required during this phase of acute illness. That conclusion was based on a retrospective analysis of neuroleptic use prior to and after use of lorazepam with neuroleptics for acute agitation (Saltzman et al. 1986). However, the potential efficacy of lorazepam in neuroleptic nonresponders has not, to our knowledge, been studied.

Clonazepam has been anecdotally reported to be a useful adjunct to neuroleptics. This has not been supported by the one controlled study to date (Karson et al. 1982).

The chapter on clozapine (Kane et al., Chapter 9, this volume) should be considered the "opening of a door" on the subject of "atypical" neuroleptics. Many pharmaceutical firms are currently developing such agents. These efforts use a variety of theoretical approaches. Some are modeled after proposed mechanisms of action of clozapine itself (5-HT_2 blockade alone or in combination with D_2 blockade, or attempted "balanced" D_1, D_2 blockade). Other approaches explore new potential mechanisms of antipsychotic effect, such as modulation of the serotonergic system via 5-HT_3 receptor blockade or antagonism of sigma opiate receptors (Coward 1989). Indeed, at the 1988 Collegium Internationale Neuro-Psychopharmacologicum meeting, preliminary data on no less than six such agents were presented. It seems likely that this massive effort will produce some new potentially important agents.

Other agents with neurobiologic effects different than those of atypical neuroleptics but with antipsychotic potential have also been studied or are in early clinical trials. Autoreceptors agonists, which decrease presynaptic activity, have been extensively studied by Tamminga and colleagues (Tamminga and Gerlack 1987, and references therein), but evidence of practical applicability has not emerged in these studies. Newer, more selective agents of this class, however, have had only limited or no clinical trials to date.

Yet another very interesting new approach to antipsychotic efficacy is the development of partial D_2 receptor agonists of such low intrinsic activity that they act as antagonists at synaptic receptors exposed to high concentrations of dopamine (which presumably mediate psychosis) yet are "recognized" as agonists by sensitive receptors, such as those regulating prolactin (Carlsson 1983). Such agents exhibit a "dualistic" agonist-antagonist profile. In preclinical studies they inhibit dopamine agonist-induced stereotypy and decrease conditioned-avoidance responding, yet cause no significant catalepsy, suppress prolactin, and behave as agonists in unilateral 6-hydroxydopamine-lesioned animals. In humans, single doses in nonschizophrenic volunteers cause sedation and prolactin elevation, yet early data from studies of 4 weeks of treatment of schizophrenic patients have to date shown no change or suppression of prolactin and lack of extrapyramidal side effects (Coward et al. 1989).

CONCLUSIONS

We are delighted that this important area is one in which such active research is now ongoing and hope that these efforts will ultimately make this volume obsolete (to the benefit of our patients). However, this is not likely to occur overnight. In the meantime, we hope this volume will be useful to the clinicians who treat these most difficult patients and to the investigators exploring this long-neglected problem.

REFERENCES

Ayd FJ Jr: Thorazine and Serpasil treatment of private neuropsychiatric patients. Am J Psychiatry 113:16–21, 1956

Bacopoulos NG, Heninger GR, Roth RH: Effects of haloperidol and probenicid on plasma and CSF dopamine metabolites in the rhesus monkey (Macacca mulatta). Life Sci 23:1805–1812, 1978

Bacopoulos NG, Hattox SE, Roth RH: 3,4-Dihydroxyphenylacetic acid and homovanillic acid in rat plasma: possible indications of central dopaminergic activity. Eur J Pharmacol 56:225–236, 1979

Bacopoulos NG, Redmond DE, Baulu J, et al: Chronic haloperidol or fluphenazine: effects on dopamine metabolism in brain, cerebrospinal fluid and plasma in Cercopithecus aethiops (Vervet monkey). J Pharmacol Exp Ther 212:1–5, 1980

Barsa J, Kline N: Combined reserpine-chlorpromazine treatment of disturbed psychotics. AMA Archives of Neurology and Psychiatry 74:280–286, 1955

Bird EG, Goss JD Jr, Denber HCB: Chlorpromazine in the treatment of mental illness: a study of 750 patients (preliminary clinical report). Am J Psychiatry 111:930, 1955

Bowers MB: Family history and CSF HVA patterns during neuroleptic treatment. Am J Psychiatry 141:296–298, 1984

Brooks GW: Experience with the use of chlorpromazine and reserpine in psychiatry. N Engl J Med 254:1119–1123, 1956

Bunney BS, Sesack SR, Silva NL: Midbrain dopaminergic systems: neurophysiology and electrophysiological pharmacology, in Psychopharmacology: The Third Generation of Progress. Edited by Meltzer HY. New York, Raven, 1987, pp 113–126

Carlsson A: Dopamine receptor agonists: intrinsic activity vs. state of receptor. J Neural Transm 57:309–315, 1983

Cole JO, Goldberg SC, Klerman GL: Phenothiazine treatment in acute schizophrenia. Arch Gen Psychiatry 10:246–261, 1964

Cole JO, Goldberg SC, Davis JM: Drugs in the treatment of psychosis: controlled studies, in Psychiatric Drugs. Edited by Solomon P. New York, Grune & Stratton, 1966, pp 153–180

Coward DM: Pharmacological approaches towards the development of atypical antipsychotics (abstract). Schizophrenia Research 2:182, 1989

Coward DM, Dixon K, Enz A, et al: Non-classical neuroleptic like properties of partial dopamine agonists (abstract). Schizophrenia Research 2:183, 1989

Crow TJ, MacMillan JF, Johnson AL, et al: The Northwick Park study of first episodes of schizophrenia, II: a randomized controlled trial of prophylactic neuroleptic treatment. Br J Psychiatry 148:120–127, 1986

Csernansky JG, Riney SJ, Yombrozo L, et al: Double blind comparison of alprazolam, diazepam and placebo for the treatment of schizophrenic negative symptoms. Arch Gen Psychiatry 45:655–659, 1988

Davila R: Plasma HVA, neuroleptics, and dopaminergic plasticity. Biol Psychiatry 25:1–3, 1989

Davis JM, Schaffer CB, Killian GA, et al: Important issues in the drug treatment of schizophrenia. Schizophr Bull 6:70–87, 1980

Davis KL, Davidson M, Mohs RC, et al: Plasma homovanillic acid concentration and the severity of schizophrenic illness. Science 227:1601–1602, 1985

Denber HCB, Bird EG: Chlorpromazine in the treatment of mental illness, IV: final results with analysis of data on 1,523 patients. Am J Psychiatry 113:972–978, 1957

Donlon P, Meadow A, Tupin J, et al: High vs. standard dosage fluphenazine HCL in acute schizophrenia. J Clin Psychiatry 39:800–804, 1978

Douyon R, Angrist B, Peselow E, et al: Neuroleptic augmentation with alprazolam: clinical effects and pharmacokinetic correlates. Am J Psychiatry 146:231–234, 1989

Ericksen S, Hurt SW, Chang S, et al: Haloperidol dose, plasma levels and clinical response: a double blind study. Psychopharmacol Bull 14(2):15–16, 1978

Friedhoff AJ: A dopamine dependent restitutive system for the maintenance of mental normalcy. Ann NY Acad Sci 463:47–52, 1986

Goldberg SC, Klerman GL, Cole JO: Changes in schizophrenic psychopathology and ward behavior as a function of phenothiazine treatment. Br J Psychiatry 111:120–123, 1965

Goldberg SC, Frosch WA, Drossman AK, et al: Prediction of response to phenothiazines in schizophrenia: a cross-validation study. Arch Gen Psychiatry 26:367–373, 1972

Guy W: ECDEU Assessment Manual for Psychopharmacology (DHEW Publ No ADM-76-338). Washington, DC, U.S. Department of Health, Education, and Welfare, 1976, pp 217–222

Hollister LE, Kim DY: Intensive treatment with haloperidol of treatment-resistant chronic schizophrenic patients. Am J Psychiatry 139:1466–1468, 1982

Kane J, Honigfeld G, Singer J, et al: Clozapine for the treatment resistant schizophrenic. Arch Gen Psychiatry 45:789–796, 1988

Karson CN, Weinberger DR, Bigelow L, et al: Clonazepam treatment of chronic schizophrenia: negative results in a double blind placebo controlled trial. Am J Psychiatry 139:1627–1628, 1982

Kendler KS, Heninger GR, Roth RH: Brain contribution to the haloperidol induced increase in plasma homovanillic acid. Eur J Phamacol 71:321–326, 1981

Kendler KS, Heninger GR, Roth RH: Influence of dopamine agonists on plasma and brain levels of homovanillic acid. Life Sci 30:2063–2069, 1982

Kinross-Wright V: Chlorpromazine treatment of mental disorders. Am J Psychiatry 111:907–912, 1955

Kolakowska T, Williams AO, Ardern M, et al: Schizophrenia with good and poor outcome, I: early clinical features, response to neuroleptics and signs of organic dysfunction. Br J Psychiatry 146:229–239, 1985

Lehmann HE, Hanrahan GE: Chlorpromazine: new inhibiting agent for psychomotor excitement and manic states. AMA Archives of Neurology and Psychiatry 71:227–237, 1954

MacMillan JF, Crow TJ, Johnson AL, et al: The Northwick Park study of first episodes of schizophrenia, III: short-term outcome in trial entrants and trial eligible patients. Br J Psychiatry 148:128–133, 1986

May PRA, Tuma AH, Yale C, et al: Schizophrenia—a follow-up study of results of treatment. Arch Gen Psychiatry 33:481–486, 1976

Overall JE, Gorham DR: The Brief Psychiatric Rating Scale. Psychol Rep 10:799–812, 1962

Pachter M: A clinical evaluation of chlorpromazine therapy in chronic schizophrenics (clinical note). Am J Psychiatry 113:931, 1957

Pickar D, Labarca R, Linnoila M, et al: Neuroleptic-induced decrease in plasma homovanillic acid and antipsychotic activity in schizophrenic patients. Science 225:954–957, 1984

Pickar D, Labarca R, Doran AR, et al: Longitudinal measurement of plasma homovanillic acid levels in schizophrenic patients. Arch Gen Psychiatry 43:669–676, 1986

Quitkin F, Rifkin A, Klein DF: Very high dose vs. standard dosage fluphenazine in schizophrenia. Arch Gen Psychiatry 32:1276–1281, 1975

Salzman C, Green A, Rodriguez-Villa F, et al: Benzodiazepine combined with neuroleptics for the management of severe disruptive behavior. Psychosomatics 27:17–21, 1986

Szatmari A: Clinical and electroencephalogram investigation on Largactil in psychosis (preliminary study). Am J Psychiatry 112:788–794, 1956

Tamminga CA, Gerlack J: New neuroleptics and experimental antipsychotics in schizophrenia, in Psychopharmacology: The Third Generation of Progress. Edited by Meltzer HY. New York, Raven, 1987, pp 1129–1140

Winkelman NW Jr: An appraisal of chlorpromazine: general principles for administration of chlorpromazine, based on experience with 1,090 patients. Am J Psychiatry 113:961–971, 1957

Wolkowitz OM, Breier A, Doran A, et al: Alprazolam augmentation of the antipsychotic effects of fluphenazine in schizophrenic patients: preliminary results. Arch Gen Psychiatry 45:664–671, 1988

Chapter 1

Characteristics of Kraepelinian Schizophrenia and Their Relation to Premorbid Sociosexual Functioning

Richard S. E. Keefe, Ph.D.
Richard C. Mohs, Ph.D.
Jeremy M. Silverman, Ph.D.
Miklos F. Losonczy, Ph.D., M.D.
Michael Davidson, M.D.
Thomas B. Horvath, M.D.
Kenneth L. Davis, M.D.

Chapter 1

Characteristics of Kraepelinian Schizophrenia and Their Relation to Premorbid Sociosexual Functioning

Impaired social adjustment in individuals with schizophrenia has been repeatedly demonstrated. Schizophrenic patients have shown more social impairment following the onset of their disorder than individuals with other psychiatric disorders and normal control subjects (Goodman et al. 1969; Rosen et al. 1980; Schooler and Paykel 1966; Serban 1975; Spitzer et al. 1970), and the level of their premorbid social adjustment has also been shown to be significantly lower than either of these groups (Lewine et al. 1978, 1980; Watt 1978; Watt et al. 1970). The severe social deterioration that often accompanies chronic, unremitting schizophrenia places a greater emotional and financial demand on society than any other component of psychiatric illness. Consequently, the most chronically deteriorated schizophrenic patients, who require either continuous hospitalization or continuous care, are most in need of study. In addition, these patients, due to the severity of their illness, may yield more information about the entire spectrum of schizophrenic disorders than any other group. Noninvasive, descriptive measures associated with social deterioration would be of value in identifying and classifying those patients who will eventually reach this severely deteriorated state. If noninvasive measures in the areas of clinical description, biology,

This work was supported by a SBRC grant #4125-020 from the General Medical Research Service of the Veterans Administration and a grant from the NIMH (MH-37922).

3

exclusion criteria, and family study (Robins and Guze 1972) could discriminate chronically deteriorated schizophrenic patients from those less deteriorated chronic schizophrenic patients whose longitudinal course includes periods of total or partial remission, initial steps toward identifying an important subgroup of schizophrenia would be taken.

One problematic aspect of identifying measures associated with severe social deterioration in schizophrenia is that, for concurrent measures, the direction of causality involved in these relationships remains uncertain. Ideally, longitudinal studies designed to assess these variables throughout the life span of a schizophrenic patient could determine the direction of causality between severe social deterioration in the end stage of schizophrenia and concurrent and prospective measures. However, in the absence of such studies, assessment of premorbid social impairment in a group of schizophrenic patients, including those with the most severe current social deterioration, could help promote an understanding of the relationship between concurrent characteristics of very poor outcome schizophrenia and social behavior before the devastating effects of frank psychosis and its treatment have emerged.

To address these issues, we conducted a two-part investigation of the characteristics of very poor outcome schizophrenia and their relation to premorbid social factors. In our first study, we compared a group of severely deteriorated schizophrenic male veterans, who for the past 5 years had been either continuously hospitalized or unable to provide themselves with necessities such as food, shelter, and clothing, to a group of other chronic schizophrenic male veterans, whose prior longitudinal course included periods of total or partial remission alternating with exacerbations requiring inpatient care. In view of the similarity between the longitudinal course of the severely deteriorated schizophrenic patients and the progressive deterioration of dementia praecox described by Kraepelin (1904), these patients were designated "Kraepelinian" schizophrenics. The Kraepelinian patients, if they were distinguishable from other chronic schizophrenic patients, would be expected to differ by diagnostic measures, such as the frequency of diagnosis of schizophrenia according to various diagnostic criteria (McGlashan 1984; Stephens et al. 1982), as well as by descriptive measures associated with poor prognosis, such as absence of response to neuroleptic treatment, time in hospital, age at onset, and level of functioning. In addition, data suggest that ventricular abnormalities (Weinberger et al. 1980), negative symptoms (Crow 1980), and family history of schizophrenia spectrum disorders (McGlashan 1986) may be other potential indicators of poor prognosis Kraepelinian schizophrenia. Our second study investigated the hypothesis that the concurrent characteristics of these Kraepelinian patients, rather than being a result of long-term social deterioration, would be associated with premorbid factors, such as poor premorbid sociosexual functioning.

METHOD

Subjects

The sample consisted of 127 male chronic schizophrenic patients with a mean ± SD age of 38.3 ±10.7 years (range, 22–65) who were admitted to the Schizophrenia Biological Research Center of the Bronx Veterans Administration Medical Center of the Mount Sinai School of Medicine, New York. All patients met criteria for definite schizophrenia or schizoaffective disorder, mainly schizophrenic, according to the Research Diagnostic Criteria (RDC) (Spitzer et al. 1978) or definite schizophrenia according to the Feighner diagnostic system (Feighner et al. 1972). Patients with chronic medical illness or substance abuse were excluded from the study. In addition to the 127 patients, 15 remitted patients were also studied. Patients were separated into three clinical groups: 15 remitted, 101 exacerbated, and 26 Kraepelinian patients. Remitted patients were all volunteers who, by definition, were not in need of hospitalization for the 3 months before admission. They received four weekly scores on the Brief Psychiatric Rating Scale (BPRS) (Overall and Gorham 1962), with a mean score of 30.0 ± 6.0 (range of less than 10 points). The Kraepelinian group had a mean score of 42.5 ± 6.7. They met the following criteria for the past 5 years: 1) either continuous hospitalization or, if living outside the hospital, complete dependence on others for necessities such as food, shelter, and clothing; 2) no useful work or employment; and 3) no evidence of a remission of symptoms. The patients in the exacerbated group had a mean BPRS score of 45.5 ± 7.7. They required hospitalization, but did not meet the criteria for the Kraepelinian group. Informed consent was obtained from the patient or from a first-degree relative if an otherwise assenting patient was unable to give true informed consent.

Diagnosis and Clinical Description

All patients were interviewed by a two-member diagnostic team that used the Schedule for Affective Disorders and Schizophrenia (SADS) (Endicott and Spitzer 1978). Team members independently determined diagnoses according to the following criteria: RDC and the Feighner system; DSM-III (American Psychiatric Association 1980);

and the "flexible" system of the International Pilot Study of Schizophrenia (Carpenter et al. 1973), Schneiderian first-rank symptoms (Schneider 1959), and Langfeldt's criteria (Langfeldt 1960). The RDC were used to determine if, in addition to schizophrenic symptoms, a patient had ever manifested a full affective syndrome, defined as a prominent mood disturbance accompanied by at least four significant affective symptoms.

Data regarding several clinical variables were obtained by two independent raters. Severity of formal thought disorder was measured by the Thought, Language and Communication Scale (Andreasen 1979). Current social and occupational functioning was measured with the Level of Functioning Scale (intraclass correlation coefficient [ICC] = 0.91, 1/67 df, $P < .001$) (Strauss and Carpenter 1974) by summing items rating the number and quality of social contacts, duration of nonhospitalization during the past year, work history in the past year, overall symptom severity in the past month, and overall "quality of life." Negative symptoms were assessed in 54 patients by determining total scores (excluding global and subjective rating scores) on the Scale for the Assessment of Negative Symptoms (Andreasen 1982) (ICC = 0.82 1/42 df, $P < .001$). In addition, negative symptoms severity scores (Rosen et al. 1984) were assessed for the entire cohort by using items on the SADS, the Thought, Language and Communication Scale, and the Level of Functioning Scale that corresponded to 16 of the 30 items on the Scale for the Assessment of Negative Symptoms. Positive symptom severity scores (Rosen et al. 1984) (ICC = 0.82, 1/74 df, $P < .001$), which estimate scores obtained from the Scale for the Assessment of Positive Symptoms (Andreasen 1984), were determined by summing SADS items rating severity of hallucinations, delusions, bizarre behavior, and positive formal thought disorder. Number of positive symptoms was determined by summing the number of RDC schizophrenic symptoms (the "A" criteria) manifested (ICC = 0.79, 1/67 df, $P < .001$). Overall severity of psychopathology was assessed by Clinical Global Impression (CGI) (Guy 1976) scores (ICC = .75, 1/67 df, $P < .001$).

Data regarding age at onset, number of psychiatric hospitalizations, total time in psychiatric hospitals, and educational level were gathered for all patients. In nearly all cases, the two best informants available were interviewed, and all medical records were reviewed to verify and supplement information gathered by the patient interview. Consensus scores and diagnoses were determined for all diagnostic and descriptive data by both team members and an independent diagnostic expert, who resolved any disagreements.

Assessment of Premorbid Social and Sexual Functioning

In a subgroup of 69 patients in the exacerbated and Kraepelinian groups, premorbid social and sexual dysfunction was assessed with the Premorbid Asocial Adjustment Scale (Gittelman-Klein and Klein 1969), which consists of seven items, each scored from 1 to 7. A set of scoring guidelines is included with each item of the scale. The premorbid asociosexual functioning item, referred to as "sociosexual adjustment" on the scale, is rated for the period of time when the patient was 16–20 years old. For each patient, ratings of premorbid asocial adjustment were obtained by two independent raters from at least two informants who had observed the patient frequently during the premorbid period. The reliability of each informant was rated on a scale of 1 (very good) to 5 (very poor); reliability ratings of 1–3 were considered adequate. In a previous report (Small et al. 1984) on a subgroup of 45 patients from this cohort, interrater reliability was found to be high for all items of the Premorbid Asocial Adjustment Scale, but agreement between informants was found to be adequate only for the premorbid asociosexual functioning item (ICC = 0.82, 1/67 df, $P < .01$). All other items of this scale did not demonstrate significant interinformant reliability. Because these data indicate that only the item on sociosexual adjustment is a reliable indicator of premorbid adjustment, and because of reports from other investigations that predic-tion from premorbid data is more successful with individual characteristics than with a comprehensive prognostic scale (Gaebel and Pietzcker 1987; Strauss and Carpenter 1974), data analysis included only the premorbid asociosexual functioning item.

Score definition for premorbid asociosexual functioning and the distribution among our 69 patients are presented in Table 1-1. The original scale included an additional rating of "homosexual involve-ment only," which was given a score of 6; "no sexual interests in either sex" was scored as a 7. Because the homosexual involvement only rating was viewed as a disruption of the quantitative nature of this measure, it was excluded from the measure, and no sexual interests was scored as a 6. The result of this transformation of the data was an ordinal scale on which increasing scores were associated with less sociosexual involvement. The one patient who was rated as having homosexual involvement only on the scale was excluded from the study. The distribution of the scores among our patients was moderately positively skewed. The mean of these scores is 2.99 ± 1.58.

Family History

Diagnostic family histories were gathered on 100 patients by a specialist in family diagnostic interviews who was blind to the premorbid functioning of the proband and whether he was considered Kraepelinian. In 55 cases, two family members were interviewed; in the other 45 cases, one family member was interviewed. A family history of schizophrenia spectrum disorders was defined as any first- or second-degree relative who met the criteria for any of the following family history RDC (Endicott et al. 1975) definite or probable diagnoses: chronic schizophrenia; schizoaffective disorder, chronic type; or unspecified functional psychosis, chronic type. Diagnosis of definite or probable schizophrenia-related personality (Kendler et al. 1984) was also used as a criterion for a family history of schizophrenia spectrum disorders. The morbid risk of schizophrenia spectrum disorders was calculated for all first-degree relatives of each patient to correct for the size of the patient's family. The Weinberg-abridged method was used to correct for an otherwise likely underestimation of risk due to the possibility that relatives who had not fully passed through the age of risk (defined as ages 15–39 for schizophrenia spectrum disorders) may yet manifest a disorder.

Treatment Response

Twenty-one Kraepelinian and 54 exacerbated patients in the sample underwent a standardized dose schedule of haloperidol to determine

Table 1-1. Assessment of premorbid asociosexual functioning score

Score	Description	N
1	Healthy interest in girls, steady close relationships with sexual intercourse or sexual play, went out with girls regularly, steady close relationships with little or no sexual play.	16
2	Went out with girls regularly, steady casual relationships with or without sexual play or intercourse.	12
3	Went out with girls regularly, passing casual relationships with or without sexual play or intercourse.	10
4	Casual occasional contact with girls with or without sexual intercourse or sexual play.	16
5	Interested in girls, but never went out on dates.	11
6	No sexual interests in either sex.	4

treatment response. All patients received 10 mg of haloperidol two times/day for 28 days. When clinically indicated, haloperidol dose was increased to 15 mg two times/day until day 36, at which time it was increased to 20 mg two times/day until day 43. BPRS and CGI scores were obtained weekly by two independent raters. Treatment response was predefined as a decrease in BPRS of at least 20% or a decrease in CGI of at least 2 points from drug-free baseline to either day 29 or to the last day of the treatment response study. The interrater reliability of BPRS change was high (ICC = .94, 1/36 df, $P < .001$).

Ventricle-Brain Ratio

Ventricle-brain ratio and lateral ventricular asymmetry were determined from computed tomography scans of the head of 72 of our patients on a high resolution Technicon 2020 scanner. This latter measure was determined by dividing the area of the left ventricle by the area of the right ventricle, resulting in the left-to-right lateral ventricular ratio. The methods for determining ventricle-brain ratio and lateral ventricular asymmetry have been described in greater detail elsewhere (Keefe et al. 1987).

RESULTS

Kraepelinian Patients

Kraepelinian schizophrenic patients were different from other chronic schizophrenic patients on several different measures. Consensus diagnoses for all patients indicated that Kraepelinian patients could be diagnosed as schizophrenic more consistently across varying diagnostic systems than other exacerbated chronic schizophrenic patients (see Table 1-2). Kraepelinian patients were diagnosed as having schizophrenia by a mean of 5.7 of the 6 diagnostic systems; exacerbated patients met criteria for schizophrenia by 4.9 of them ($t = -2.62$, 89.16 df, $P < .01$).

Kraepelinian patients differed from exacerbated schizophrenic patients by several other clinical measures. As demonstrated in Table 1-3, Kraepelinian patients had more severe formal thought disorder, as measured by the Thought, Language and Communication Scale ($P < .002$), and higher negative symptoms severity scores, as assessed by items on the SADS, the Thought, Language and Communication Scale, and the Level of Functioning Scale that corresponded to 16 of the 30 items on the Scale for the Assessment of Negative Symptoms ($P < .01$). Among the 54 patients for whom total scores on the Scale for the Assessment of Negative Symptoms were determined, there was

Table 1-2. Comparison between Kraepelinian and exacerbated groups for positive diagnosis of schizophrenia for six diagnostic systems

Group	N	Research Diagnostic Criteria[a]		DSM-III[b]		International Pilot Study of Schizophrenia[c]				Feighner's criteria[d]		Langfeldt's criteria		Schneider's first-rank symptoms	
						5		6							
		n	%	n	%	n	%	n	%	n	%	n	%	n	%
Kraepelinian	26	25	96	26	100	26*	100	24**	92	23**	88	23	88	20	77
Exacerbated	101	87	87	94	94	82	82	73	73	71	71	97	97	80	80

[a]15 schizoaffective patients considered negative. [b]7 schizophrenic patients considered negative. [c]5 and 6 refer to the number of symptoms present from the criteria (of a possible 11 symptoms). [d]13 "probable" schizophrenic patients considered negative.
*P < .01. **P < .05.

Table 1-3. Mean ± SD significant differences between Kraepelinian and exacerbated schizophrenic patients

Variable	Kraepelinian (N = 26)	Exacerbated (N = 101)	t	df	P
Age (years)	45.1 ± 10.6	34.9 ± 10.1	4.67	125	.001
Months in hospital	116.2 ± 102.8	36.7 ± 52.8	4.76	125	.001
LFS scores	14.7 ± 3.0	20.4 ± 6.0	4.84	123	.001
TLC total scores	18.0 ± 8.8	12.3 ± 8.0	3.24	125	.002
Negative symptoms scores	38.5 ± 9.7	31.8 ± 12.3	2.72	123	.01
SANS total scores	48.4 ± 12.3	41.4 ± 16.8	1.68	92	.10

Note. LFS = Level of Functioning Scale; TLC = Thought, Language and Communication Scale; SANS = Scale for the Assessment of Negative Symptoms.

a trend for Kraepelinian patients to have higher total scores ($P < .10$). Kraepelinian patients also had worse social and occupational functioning, as measured by the Level of Functioning Scale; they had spent more time in psychiatric hospitals, and they were older ($P < .001$ for all measures). Positive symptoms, as determined by the positive symptom severity score from SADS items and by the number of RDC "A" criteria met, revealed no significant differences between the two groups. Kraepelinian patients also did not differ significantly from exacerbated schizophrenic patients on measures of age at onset (24.5 versus 23.1), education (11.3 versus 12.2 years), premorbid asociosexual functioning (3.1 versus 2.9), and number of hospitalizations (7.8 versus 6.5).

Kraepelinian patients had significantly more cases of schizophrenia spectrum disorders in their first- or second-degree relatives than non-Kraepelinian schizophrenia patients ($P < .05$), and their first-degree relatives had a higher morbid risk of schizophrenia spectrum disorders than the first-degree relatives of the non-Kraepelinian schizophrenic patients ($P < .05$) (Table 1-4).

Because of demonstrated differences in age between the Kraepelinian and non-Kraepelinian groups and the possible effect of age on lateral ventricular measures, the Kraepelinian patients were compared to a group of age-matched chronic schizophrenic patients. There was a significant difference between the two groups in lateral ventricular asymmetry. The mean left/right ventricle ratio was 1.17 ± 0.22 for the 15 Kraepelinian patients versus 0.99 ± 0.18 for the 15 age-matched non-Kraepelinian schizophrenic patients ($t = -2.53$; 28 df, $P < .02$). All but two of the patients in this study were right-handed. In a preliminary study of 60 patients, handedness showed no relationship to lateral ventricular asymmetry. No significant difference was found in ventricle-brain ratio between the Kraepelinian and non-Kraepelinian schizophrenic patients (6.4 versus 5.9).

Response to haloperidol was defined as 1) a decrease in BPRS scores of at least 20% from baseline to either day 29 or to the last day of the study or 2) a two-point decrease in CGI scores from baseline to either day 29 or to the last day of the study. None of the 21 Kraepelinian schizophrenic patients who participated in the treatment response study demonstrated a response to haloperidol treatment; 24 of the 54 exacerbated patients did respond ($\chi^2 = 22.4$, df = 1, $P < .001$). Eighteen Kraepelinian patients were also compared to a group of 18 exacerbated patients matched by mean baseline BPRS score (41.7 ± 7.3 versus 42.3 ± 5.8). Six of these exacerbated patients met criteria for treatment response, which was significantly different from the Kraepelinian group ($\chi^2 = 7.2$, df = 1, $P < .01$).

Table 1-4. Family history of schizophrenia and first-degree relative morbid risk: Kraepelinian versus non-Kraepelinian schizophrenic patients

Group	N	Family history of first- and second-degree relatives		N of first-degree relatives		Lifetimes of risk	Schizophrenia spectrum disorder cases	Morbid risk[b,c]
		Positive[a]	Negative	Age 15–39	Age 40 +			
Kraepelinian	20	12	8	24	71	83	15	.181
Non-Kraepelinian	80	27	53	176	217	305	31	.102

[a]$\chi^2 = 4.63$, $P = <.05$. [b]$Z = 1.98$, $P < .05$. [c]Age-corrected likelihood of a schizophrenia spectrum disorder diagnosis in first-degree relatives.

Kraepelinian Characteristics and Premorbid Asociosexual Functioning

Higher premorbid asociosexual functioning scores, suggesting lower levels of social and sexual activity before the onset of schizophrenia, were found to correlate significantly with several characteristics of Kraepelinian schizophrenia. Higher premorbid asociosexual functioning scores were associated with lower levels of current social and occupational functioning and severity of symptoms, as determined by the Level of Functioning Scale total scores ($r = -.26$; 67 df, $P < .03$), current number of social contacts ($r = -.51$; 67 df, $P < .001$), and quality of social contacts ($r = -.34$; 67 df, $P < .005$). Higher premorbid asociosexual functioning scores also correlated significantly with greater overall severity of psychopathology, as assessed by the CGI ($r = .25$, 67 df, $P < .05$); a greater severity of negative symptoms, as assessed by negative symptom severity scores ($r = .32$, 67 df, $P < .01$); and fewer positive symptoms, as determined by the number of RDC schizophrenia symptoms manifested ($r = -.29$, 67 df, $P < .03$). The correlation between premorbid asociosexual functioning scores and severity of negative symptoms as determined by the Scale for the Assessment of Negative Symptoms total scores was not significant. However, scores were available for only 36 of the patients in this study, which resulted in a considerable loss of statistical power for this analysis. There was no significant correlation between premorbid asociosexual functioning scores and severity of positive symptoms as determined by scores estimating the Scale for the Assessment of Positive Symptoms from SADS items. Premorbid asociosexual functioning scores were not significantly correlated with age, age of onset, number of psychiatric hospitalizations, total time in psychiatric hospitals, number of years ill, or educational level. Premorbid asociosexual functioning was not significantly related to whether a patient was Kraepelinian.

Premorbid asociosexual functioning scores correlated significantly with the degree of left-to-right lateral ventricular asymmetry, which was calculated by dividing the mean area of the left ventricle by the mean area of the right ventricle ($r = .28$, 51 df, $P < .05$). Thus greater premorbid sociosexual impairment was associated with greater left-to-right lateral ventricular asymmetry. Ventricle-brain ratio was not significantly correlated with premorbid asociosexual functioning scores.

Symptom improvement during haloperidol treatment, measured in 38 patients by the decrease in total BPRS score from baseline to the last day of the study, covaried for baseline BPRS score, was not significantly related to premorbid asociosexual functioning score.

DISCUSSION

A group of severely deteriorated Kraepelinian schizophrenic patients, who for the past 5 years were either continuously hospitalized or completely dependent on others for their survival, differed from other chronic schizophrenic patients on a number of measures. They more consistently received a diagnosis of schizophrenia across cross-sectional and longitudinal diagnostic criteria, had more severe negative symptoms, had a greater morbid risk for schizophrenia spectrum disorders in their first-degree relatives, had a greater left-to-right asymmetry of their lateral cerebral ventricles compared to a group of other age-matched chronic schizophrenic patients, and had less of a prospective response to a standard dose of haloperidol. Severity of positive symptoms, however, did not distinguish Kraepelinian schizophrenic patients from other chronic schizophrenic patients.

Poor premorbid sociosexual functioning was found to be associated with several of the concurrent characteristics of Kraepelinian schizophrenia, including greater current severity of negative symptoms, greater overall severity of psychopathology, worse current social and occupational functioning, and greater left-to-right lateral ventricular asymmetry, but not significantly associated with symptom improvement during haloperidol treatment. Poor premorbid sociosexual functioning was also associated with fewer positive symptoms. Premorbid sociosexual functioning was not significantly different between Kraepelinian schizophrenic patients and other schizophrenic patients.

A more detailed discussion of the specific findings from previous analyses of these data involving smaller sample sizes can be found elsewhere (Keefe et al. 1987, 1989). One finding from this study deserves particular attention. Kraepelinian patients demonstrated a significantly greater left-to-right ratio of their cerebral ventricles. This characteristic was also found to be significantly associated with poor premorbid sociosexual impairment. These two findings provide antecedent and concurrent support for the notion that severe social impairment in schizophrenia may be related to defects in brain structure (Weinberger et al. 1980; Williams et al. 1985). These data are also consistent with previous reports of an association between the absence of normal left occipital asymmetry and greater psychopathology in schizophrenic patients (Luchins and Meltzer 1983), as well as reports of schizophrenic patients in general with an increased incidence of reversal of normal anatomic asymmetries (Luchins et al.

1979, 1982), anterior left hemisphere atrophy (Golden et al. 1981), diminished left caudate function on metabolic positron emission tomography scan (Buchsbaum et al. 1982), and postmortem studies finding decreased cortical width in the left parahippocampal gyrus (Stevens 1984). Hence, the purported left-sided brain abnormality in schizophrenia may be related to premorbid and concurrent social deterioration. In the absence of replication from other investigators, this relationship should be viewed cautiously, particularly since some degree of lateral ventricular asymmetry has been reported in a group of healthy, nonschizophrenic subjects (Schwartz et al. 1985).

The correlation of current negative symptoms, social impairment, and overall level of current psychopathology with poor premorbid sociosexual adjustment is consistent with the notion that Kraepelinian schizophrenic patients, those with the worst social outcome, differ from other schizophrenic patients not as a result of social deterioration following the onset of their psychosis, but due to dispositional factors. The etiologic relationship of prepsychotic sociosexual functioning and schizophrenic outcome is difficult to specify because asociality prior to the onset of schizophrenia is often indistinguishable from early onset of illness manifested as social impairment during the prodromal period. Poor sociosexual adjustment during adolescence in schizophrenic patients can be distinguished from manifestations of the illness only if diagnostic criteria that require psychotic symptoms are used. Kraepelin's (1904) description of the course of dementia praecox focused on the notion that the core features of the illness are the enduring negative symptoms or deficit traits that often precede psychosis for years and have been considered by others to be the symptoms most characteristic of schizophrenia (Bleuler 1908). Early sociosexual impairment of some schizophrenic patients could be either part of their premorbid personalities or a vulnerability factor to the disorder, but it is possible that at least a few patients had sociosexual difficulties during the prepsychotic period as a result of an early onset of schizophrenia. For the latter cases, the relationship between early sociosexual and current social impairment is more of a reflection of the stability of poor social functioning throughout the course of the schizophrenic illness than it is an indication of a predictor of current functioning based on the assessment of an unafflicted premorbid personality. This interpretation of the data suggests that patients who demonstrate an earlier onset of negative symptoms, such as sociosexual withdrawal, are more likely to demonstrate severe social withdrawal in the later stages of their illness. Hence, regardless of whether sociosexual impairment prior to the onset of psychosis is viewed as part of a schizophrenic individual's predisposition to the illness or as an early expression of the disorder, the data presented in this study are consistent with the notion that greater social deterioration in the end stage of schizophrenia is a result of predisposing factors.

Although premorbid sociosexual impairment was associated with several measures of current social functioning, it was not found to be significantly different between Kraepelinian and other schizophrenic patients. This apparent inconsistency among the constellation of findings reported in this study may be accounted for by the low statistical power available for this analysis due to the relatively small number of Kraepelinian patients for whom premorbid data were collected, or by the possible entry of patients into the non-Kraepelinian group who were severely deteriorated at the time of study but had not yet met the criteria for Kraepelinian schizophrenia for the full 5-year period required.

In summary, Kraepelinian schizophrenic patients, who are fully dependent on others for the necessities of life, were found to differ from other chronic schizophrenic patients with respect to antecedent, concurrent, and prospective measures. Several concurrent measures that differentiated Kraepelinian schizophrenic patients from other schizophrenic patients were found to be associated with premorbid sociosexual impairment. These data are consistent with the notion that the concurrent characteristics of very poor outcome schizophrenic patients are not solely a result of the chronicity of these patients, but rather are associated with antecedent factors.

The heterogeneity of schizophrenic symptomatology has frequently been understood as a reflection of the various predisposing factors and pathways to the disorder (Bleuler 1908). The differences found in the group of Kraepelinian schizophrenic patients in this study raise the question of whether schizophrenic patients with the worst outcome, who are most consistently given a diagnosis of schizophrenia by varying diagnostic systems, and thus most clearly represent the "core of schizophrenia," reach this deteriorated state by multiple insult. Thus a greater number of predisposing factors to schizophrenia, including premorbid social factors, greater genetic-familial loading, and structural abnormalities, may directly relate to a more deteriorating course of illness. Although much additional work is necessary to determine whether Kraepelinian schizophrenic patients are a distinct and valid subgroup of schizophrenia or a category of patients who are a part of a continuum of chronicity and severity, the elaboration of the biological, psychophysiologic, and phenomenological aspects of patients who are functionally disabled for an extended period of time is a potentially important area of study.

REFERENCES

American Psychiatric Association: Diagnostic and Statistical Manual of Mental Disorders, 3rd Edition. Washington, DC, American Psychiatric Association, 1980

Andreasen NC: Thought, language and communication disorders: clinical assessment, definition of terms, and evaluation of their reliability. Arch Gen Psychiatry 36:1315–1321, 1979

Andreasen NC: Negative symptoms in schizophrenia. Arch Gen Psychiatry 39:784–788, 1982

Andreasen NC: The Scale for the Assessment of Positive Symptoms (SAPS). Iowa City, IA, University of Iowa, 1984

Bleuler E: Dementia Praecox or the Group of Schizophrenias (1908). Translated by Zinkin J. New York, International Universities Press, 1950

Buchsbaum MS, Ingvar DH, Kessler R, et al: Cerebral glucography with positron tomography: use in normal subjects and in patients with schizophrenia. Arch Gen Psychiatry 39:251–259, 1982

Carpenter WT, Strauss JS, Bartko JJ: Flexible system for the diagnosis of schizophrenia: a report from the International Pilot Study of Schizophrenia. Science 182:1275–1278, 1973

Crow TJ: Molecular pathology of schizophrenia: more than one disease process? Br Med J 280:1–9, 1980

Endicott J, Spitzer RL: A diagnostic review: the Schedule for Affective Disorders and Schizophrenia. Arch Gen Psychiatry 35:837–844, 1978

Endicott J, Andreasen NC, Spitzer RL: Family History: Research Diagnostic Criteria. New York, New York State Psychiatric Institute, 1975

Feighner JP, Robins E, Guze SB, et al: Diagnostic criteria for use in psychiatric research. Arch Gen Psychiatry 26:57–63, 1972

Gaebel W, Pietzcker A: Prospective study of course of illness in schizophrenia, II: prediction of outcome. Schizophr Bull 13:299–306, 1987

Gittelman-Klein R, Klein DF: Premorbid asocial adjustment and prognosis in schizophrenia. J Psychiatr Res 7:35–53, 1969

Golden CJ, Graber B, Coffman F, et al: Structural brain deficits in schizophrenia: identification by computed tomographic scan density measurements. Arch Gen Psychiatry 38:1014–1017, 1981

Goodman SP, Schulthorpe WB, Euve M, et al: Social dysfunction among psychiatric and non-psychiatric outpatients. Journal of the Geriatric Society 17:694–700, 1969

Guy W (ed): ECDEU Assessment Manual for Psychopharmacology, Revised (DHEW Publ No ADM-76-338). Rockville, MD, National Institute of Mental Health, 1976

Keefe RSE, Mohs RC, Losonczy MF, et al: Characteristics of very poor outcome schizophrenia. Am J Psychiatry 144:889–895, 1987

Keefe RSE, Mohs RC, Davidson M, et al: Kraepelinian schizophrenia: a subgroup of schizophrenia? Psychopharmacol Bull 24:56–61, 1988

Kendler KS, Masterson CM, Ungaro R, et al: A family history study of schizophrenia-related personality disorders. Am J Psychiatry 141:424–427, 1984

Kraepelin E: Lectures on Clinical Psychiatry. London, Bailliere, Tendall, & Cox, 1904

Langfeldt G: Diagnosis and prognosis in schizophrenia. Proc R Soc Lond [Biol] 53:1047–1051, 1960

Lewine RRJ, Watt NF, Fryer JH: A study of childhood social competence, adult premorbid competence, and psychiatric outcome in three schizophrenic subtypes. J Abnorm Psychol 87:294–302, 1978

Lewine RRJ, Watt NF, Prentky RA, et al: Childhood social competence in functionally disordered psychiatric patients and in normals. J Abnorm Psychol 89:132–138, 1980

Luchins DJ, Meltzer HY: A blind controlled study of occipital cerebral asymmetry in schizophrenia. Psychiatry Res 10:87–92, 1983

Luchins DJ, Weinberger DR, Wyatt RJ: Schizophrenia: evidence of a subgroup with reversed cerebral asymmetry. Arch Gen Psychiatry 36:1309–1311, 1979

Luchins DJ, Weinberger DR, Wyatt RJ: Schizophrenia and cerebral asymmetry detected by computed tomography. Am J Psychiatry 139:753–757, 1982

McGlashan TH: Testing four diagnostic systems for schizophrenia. Arch Gen Psychiatry 41:141–144, 1984

McGlashan TH: Predictors of shorter-, medium-, and longer-term outcome in schizophrenia. Am J Psychiatry 143:50–55, 1986

Overall JE, Gorham DR: The Brief Psychiatric Rating Scale. Psychol Rep 10:799–812, 1962

Robins E, Guze SB: Establishment of diagnostic validity in psychiatric illness: its application to schizophrenia. Am J Psychiatry 126:983–987, 1972

Rosen AJ, Tureff SE, Paruna JH, et al: Pharmacotherapy of schizophrenia and affective disorders: behavioral correlates of diagnostic and demographic variables. J Abnorm Psychol 89:373–389, 1980

Rosen WG, Mohs RC, Johns CA, et al: Positive and negative symptoms in schizophrenia. Psychiatry Res 13:277–284, 1984

Schneider K: Klinische Psychopathologie, 5th Edition. New York, Grune & Stratton, 1959

Schooler C, Paykel D: The overt behavior of chronic schizophrenics and its relationship to their internal state and personal history. Psychiatry 29:67–77, 1966

Schwartz M, Creasy N, Grady CL, et al: Computed tomography analysis of brain morphometries in 30 healthy men, aged 21 to 81 years. Arch Neurol 17:146–157, 1985

Serban G: Relationship of mental status, functioning, and stress to readmission of schizophrenics. British Journal of Social and Clinical Psychology 14:291–301, 1975

Small NE, Mohs RC, Halperin R, et al: A study of the reliability of reported premorbid adjustment in schizophrenic patients. Biol Psychiatry 19:203–211, 1984

Spitzer RL, Endicott J, Fleiss JL, et al: The Psychiatric Status Schedule: a technique for evaluating psychopathology and impairment in role functioning. Arch Gen Psychiatry 23:41–55, 1970

Spitzer RL, Endicott J, Robins E: Research Diagnostic Criteria (RDC), 3rd Edition. New York, New York State Psychiatric Institute, 1978

Stephens JH, Astrup C, Carpenter WT, et al: A comparison of nine systems to diagnose schizophrenia. Psychiatry Res 6:127–143, 1982

Stevens JR: Schizophrenia and the brain at the 1984 winter workshop, Davos, Switzerland (letter). Arch Gen Psychiatry 41:816–817, 1984

Strauss JS, Carpenter WT: The prediction of outcome in schizophrenia, II: relationships between predictor and outcome variables. Arch Gen Psychiatry 31:37–42, 1974

Watt NF: Patterns of childhood social development in adult schizophrenics. Arch Gen Psychiatry 35:160–165, 1978

Watt NF, Stolorow R, Lubensky A, et al: School adjustment and behavior of children hospitalized for schizophrenia as adults. Am J Orthopsychiatry 40:637–657, 1970

Weinberger DR, Bigelow LB, Kleinman GE, et al: Cerebral ventricular enlargement in chronic schizophrenia: association with a poor response to treatment. Arch Gen Psychiatry 37:11–13, 1980

Williams AO, Reveley MA, Kolakowska T, et al: Ventricular enlargement in schizophrenia: relation to positive and negative symptoms. Am J Psychiatry 139:297–302, 1985

Chapter 2

Catecholamine Metabolites in Plasma as Correlates of Neuroleptic Response

Malcolm B. Bowers, Jr., M.D.

Chapter 2

Catecholamine Metabolites in Plasma as Correlates of Neuroleptic Response

The investigation of catecholamine metabolites in plasma as possible indicators of central catecholamine function has become active in the past decade or so. Using sensitive gas chromatographic-mass spectrometric methods for homovanillic acid (HVA) and 3-methoxy-4-hydroxyphenethyleneglycol (MHPG), Maas et al. (1979a, 1979b, 1980a, 1980b) published a series of studies in which they assessed central catecholaminergic activity in humans and in monkeys by quantifying differences in arterial and venous blood for HVA and MHPG. Some preclinical studies had indicated that plasma measures might be a reliable indicator of brain activity. In the rat, for example, dopamine agonists lowered plasma HVA whereas haloperidol increased it (Kendler et al. 1981, 1982). In addition, debrisoquin, a peripheral inhibitor of monoamine oxidase, did not significantly affect these changes, indicating that they were of central origin. Attempts to reproduce these results in primates and in humans, however, have met with somewhat conflicting results (Bacopoulos et al. 1980). In humans, the effect of apomorphine on plasma HVA is in doubt (Cutler et al. 1982; Davidson et al. 1985; Scheinin et al. 1985), while the ability of neuroleptics to increase plasma HVA appears supported by the data thus far (Bacopoulos et al. 1978; Davidson et al. 1987a, 1987b; Davila et al. 1988; Harris et al. 1984). However, the increase in HVA in plasma following clinical doses of neuroleptics seems more muted and transient than corresponding changes in animal brain or human cerebrospinal fluid (CSF).

Thus the new analytic methodologies have paved the way for studies of plasma HVA and MHPG in clinical conditions despite the lack of agreement as to the source of these compounds. Several methods, including the debrisoquin technique, have been studied as ways to enhance the contribution to plasma from the central nervous system. Kopin et al. (1988) and Maas et al. (1988) presented innovative studies. Other issues related to the reliability and validity of plasma measures have also been addressed, including the stability of repeat measures over time (Baker et al. 1988) and the effects of diet (Davidson et al. 1987a, 1987b; Mignot et al. 1988), physical activity (Kendler et al. 1983), and diurnal changes (Riddle et al. 1987).

In recent years, a number of reports have appeared in which plasma HVA and MHPG levels were assessed in relation to clinical aspects of the psychotic disorders, primarily symptoms and response to neuroleptic treatment. In this review, I will focus primarily on the use of plasma HVA and MHPG as correlates of neuroleptic response. Since neuroleptic drugs appear to affect catecholamine systems, it seems reasonable to evaluate markers of catecholamine activity in relation to neuroleptic response. Neuroleptic response may be an important clinical variable in its own right from a pharmacologic perspective. That is, the response to neuroleptic treatment may be one empirical approach to biological classification in the psychotic disorders. In addition, there are some data to suggest that neuroleptic response may be of longer-term prognostic significance (Bartkó et al. 1987; Nedopil et al. 1983; Singh 1976; Van Putten et al. 1981).

LITERATURE SURVEY

All the studies cited in this review employed, at a minimum, overnight fasting conditions to avoid dietary influences and measured free plasma HVA or MHPG by gas chromatography-mass spectrometry or high-performance liquid chromatography. Some of the earliest studies of plasma HVA and MHPG in psychotic disorders were performed in association with CSF measures in which probenecid was used to block the egress of acid metabolites from CSF (Heninger et al. 1979). (These studies indicated that probenecid also increased plasma HVA, presumably by blocking the renal transport mechanism for weak organic acids. It is likely that defects in this system, possibly associated with aging, would be one possible source of variance in plasma HVA, for example.) Some pretreatment correlations between plasma HVA and positive psychotic symptoms were noted, and suggestive relationships to changing intensity of symptoms in a few individual subjects were also observed (Bowers et al. 1980).

These studies were followed by surveys on a larger scale in clinical populations. Our group initially reported elevated plasma HVA in newly admitted female psychotics and some suggestive indication that those patients with elevated pretreatment HVA responded more favorably to neuroleptic treatment (Bowers et al. 1983). We subsequently found that elevations in HVA or MHPG prior to treatment were associated with a favorable early neuroleptic response in both men and women and that good responders tended to show a decrease in HVA and MHPG over a 2–3-week period of neuroleptic treatment (Bowers et al. 1984, 1986). Our patients were newly admitted psychotic patients with a variety of DSM-III (American Psychiatric Association 1980) diagnoses, all requiring neuroleptic treatment. These correlations of pretreatment HVA and MHPG with early response have never been greater than approximately .40–.50 in these or subsequent studies of ours, largely because a number of patients in our samples without elevated pretreatment values have also had good responses. By contrast, however, a patient with elevated pretreatment values has almost always in our experience, had a favorable early response. We have determined, in subsequent work, that plasma neuroleptic levels are not responsible for these findings.

The patterns of HVA and MHPG response to neuroleptics that we observed in plasma seemed somewhat different from those that we had seen in CSF (Bowers and Heninger 1981). In CSF, using the probenecid technique, we described patterns of "tolerance" and "no tolerance" for CSF HVA during neuroleptic treatment, the former pattern having been observed earlier by Post and Goodwin (1975). In the tolerance group, we found distinct mean elevations in CSF HVA at an average of 10 days (although we did not have pretreatment measures) and a decline by average day 32. In the no tolerance group, we measured a comparably increased value for HVA at 10 days, but an even greater mean increase at 30 days. In the majority of patients (15 of 24) at 10 days, values for CSF HVA ranged from 180 to 397 ng/ml, clearly elevated in our experience, even controlling for levels of probenecid in CSF. The point here in relation to our plasma studies is that we have not seen elevations in plasma HVA during neuroleptic treatment of comparable magnitude or duration to those seen in CSF. However, others have found reliable initial increases in plasma HVA during neuroleptic treatment. Harris et al. (1984), Davidson et al. (1987a, 1987b), and Davila et al. (1988) reported increases in plasma HVA as early as 1–4 days from the onset of neuroleptic treatment. Despite the differences in the CSF and plasma studies, there is one major point of convergence—namely, the observation that those patients who improve most appear to do so in association with a *fall* in CSF HVA or plasma HVA and MHPG, relative to values before or in the first few days of neuroleptic treatment. (For an excellent review, see Pickar 1988.) Although this decline does not usually achieve values below baseline, it is generally consistent with the observation of Bunney and Grace (1978), who described a progressive inactivation of dopaminergic neuronal function in the midbrain in the course of continued neuroleptic administration to rats. It is noteworthy in this context that concomitant lithium administration appeared to uncouple the relationship between a decline in CSF HVA and neuroleptic response; that is, lithium seemed to prevent the "tolerance pattern," but patients improved as much or more when it was added to haloperidol (Sternberg et al. 1983).

Initially, Pickar et al. (1984) and Davis et al. (1985) reported increases in plasma HVA in association with the severity of positive symptoms in schizophrenic patients undergoing acute psychotic exacerbation. Pickar et al. (1984, 1986) also found predominantly a decline in plasma HVA over 5 weeks of treatment with fluphenazine. Davila et al. (1988) found that the *increase* in plasma HVA from baseline to day 4 of neuroleptic treatment as well as the *decrease* in plasma HVA from day 4 to day 28 of treatment were related to improvement. Chang et al. (1988) reported different plasma HVA patterns in good responders as compared to poor responders treated with haloperidol for 6 weeks. The good responders showed a progressive decline in plasma HVA over this period; the poor responders showed an initial increase at 1–2 weeks, with a modest decline thereafter. These patterns are similar to the ones we previously observed (Bowers et al. 1984).

The findings thus far published relating plasma HVA and MHPG to neuroleptic response are summarized in Table 2-1. It is apparent from the table that the greatest consensus thus far lies in the pattern of decline in plasma HVA being associated with a favorable neuroleptic response. Consistent with this general pattern is the report of

Table 2-1. Plasma HVA and MHPG: correlation with neuroleptic treatment response

Research group	Metabolite	Correlation
Bowers	HVA, MHPG	Pretreatment HVA or MHPG
Pickar	HVA	with treatment response
Davila	HVA	Initial increase in HVA with treatment response
Pickar	HVA	Decline in HVA or MHPG
Bowers	HVA, MHPG	during treatment with
Davila	HVA	treatment response
Chang	HVA	

Note. HVA = homovanillic acid; MHPG = 3-methoxy-4-hydroxyphenethyleneglycol.

Wolkowitz et al. (1988), which indicated that plasma HVA declined initially in those patients whose neuroleptic treatment response was most favorably augmented by alprazolam.

CRITIQUE

The studies cited in this review have not been identical in design. Some have used schizophrenic patients only, whose duration of illness varied substantially, and others have employed a variety of patients with nonorganic psychotic diagnoses. Some have been able to maintain patients drug-free for more than a week; others have not. Because several groups have not used fixed-dose neuroleptic treatment and measurement of plasma levels, it becomes difficult in those instances to separate pharmacodynamic from pharmacokinetic influences on treatment response. Perhaps the single factor contributing to noncomparability between studies has been time of measurement. Particularly in the first few days of treatment, sampling times have varied. Time for assessment of treatment response has also varied from 10 days to 6 weeks.

Obviously the optimal design for such studies depends on one's goals. If the purpose is to demonstrate clear pharmacodynamic differences in subjects that might be reflected in plasma catecholamine metabolite measures, then one would prefer a narrow diagnostic and age range, a washout period of at least 2 weeks, a fixed neuroleptic plasma range (obtained by adjustment after a test dose), and reliable treatment response measures at several points in time. If the purpose is to test the usefulness of plasma HVA and MHPG for informing the actual clinical treatment of psychotic disorders, then less uniformity on some of these items would not only be acceptable but even desirable.

One hypothesis seems to emerge at the clinical level—namely, that plasma HVA, and perhaps MHPG, might be useful in monitoring the course of treatment for acute psychosis. As with the dexamethasone suppression test, not all psychotic patients will be found to have abnormal (elevated) values, but for those who do, the data thus far suggest that successful treatment will produce a decline to a normal range or below. Further by analogy with the dexamethasone suppression test, in our experience, the clinical diagnosis of psychosis may be difficult, even occult, in a number of instances, and the presence of an elevated plasma HVA prior to treatment has been helpful and associated with successful treatment with neuroleptic drugs.

At the level of mechanism there are a number of interesting questions that remain to be addressed. As noted above, the renal excretion mechanism for weak organic acids can be a source of variation for plasma HVA. Although methods may be devised for assessing these variations in excretion, they may have their own difficulties, if the experience with the use of probenecid in CSF studies is at all informative. In addition, it is not yet clear to what degree the clinical changes that have been observed in plasma levels are due to input from central or peripheral sources. It is further possible that plasma HVA may have its origin in noradrenergic neurons (Scheinin, 1986). In this regard, our experience suggests that some psychotic patients have distinct elevations in both plasma HVA and MHPG, while others have increases in either HVA or MHPG only. The possibility that these represent distinct patient groups needs to be pursued.

CONCLUSION

There is certainly sufficient promise to encourage further work from the studies cited here. It is reassuring that a decline in plasma HVA and MHPG seems to be emerging as a pattern after 2 weeks or so of successful neuroleptic treatment, for such a pattern seems consistent with preclinical information. The correlations prior to treatment and in the first week of treatment require further study. It may be that pretreatment plasma HVA and MHPG values are characteristic of biological subgroups in the psychotic spectrum. It is also possible that plasma HVA and MHPG measures might be useful adjuncts to the clinical management of patients undergoing neuroleptic treatment, particularly those in whom the symptoms of psychosis are relatively hidden.

REFERENCES

American Psychiatric Association: Diagnostic and Statistical Manual of Mental Disorders, 3rd Edition. Washington, DC, American Psychiatric Association, 1980

Bacopoulos NG, Heninger GR, Roth RH: Effects of haloperidol and probenecid upon plasma and CSF dopamine metabolites in the rhesus monkey (macacca mulatta). Life Sci 23:1805–1812, 1978

Bacopoulos NG, Redmond DE, Baulu J, et al: Chronic haloperidol or fluphenazine: effects on dopamine metabolism in brain, cerebrospinal fluid, and plasma of Cercopithecus Aethiops (Vervet monkey). J Pharmacol Exp Ther 212:1–5, 1980

Baker NJ, Adler LE, Waldo M, et al: Reproducibility of the measurement of plasma noradrenergic and dopaminergic metabolites in normal subjects. Psychiatry Res 23:119–130, 1988

Bartkó G, Herczeg I, Békésy M: Predicting outcome of neuroleptic treatment on the basis of subjective response and early clinical improvement. J Clin Psychiatry 48:363–365, 1987

Bowers MB Jr, Heninger GR: Cerebrospinal fluid homovanillic acid patterns during neuroleptic treatment. Psychiatry Res 4:285–290, 1981

Bowers MB Jr, Heninger GR, Sternberg D, et al: Clinical processes and central dopaminergic activity in psychotic disorders. Communications in Psychopharmacology 4:177–188, 1980

Bowers MB Jr, Swigar ME, Jatlow PI: Sex differences in plasma homovanillic acid in acute psychosis. N Engl J Med 308:845–846, 1983

Bowers MB Jr, Swigar ME, Jatlow PI, et al: Plasma catecholamine metabolites and early response to haloperidol. J Clin Psychiatry 45:248–251, 1984

Bowers MB Jr, Swigar ME, Jatlow PI, et al: Early neuroleptic response in psychotic men and women: correlation with plasma HVA and MHPG. Compr Psychiatry 27:181–185, 1986

Bunney BS, Grace AA: Acute and chronic haloperidol treatment: comparison of effects on nigral dopaminergic cell activity. Life Sci 23:1717–1728, 1978

Chang W-H, Chen T-Y, Lee C-F, et al: Plasma homovanillic acid levels and subtyping of schizophrenia. Psychiatry Res 23:239–244, 1988

Cutler NR, Jeste DV, Karoum F, et al: Low-dose apomorphine reduces serum homovanillic acid in schizophrenic patients. Life Sci 30:753–756, 1982

Davidson M, Kendler KS, Davis BM, et al: Apomorphine has no effect on plasma HVA in schizophrenic patients. Psychiatry Res 16:95–99, 1985

Davidson M, Giordani AB, Mohs RC, et al: Control of exogenous factors affecting plasma homovanillic acid concentration. Psychiatry Res 20:307–312, 1987a

Davidson M, Giordani AB, Mohs RC, et al: Short-term haloperidol administration acutely elevates human plasma HVA concentration (letter). Arch Gen Psychiatry 44:189, 1987b

Davila R, Manero E, Zumarraga M, et al: Plasma homovanillic acid as a predictor of response to neuroleptics. Arch Gen Psychiatry 45:564–567, 1988

Davis KL, Davidson M, Mohs RC, et al: Plasma homovanillic acid concentration and the severity of schizophrenic illness. Science 227:1601–1602, 1985

Harris PQ, Brown SJ, Friedman MJ, et al: Plasma drug and homovanillic acid levels in psychotic patients receiving neuroleptics. Biol Psychiatry 19:849–860, 1984

Heninger G, Bacopoulos N, Roth R, et al: Plasma and CSF dopamine metabolites in psychiatric patients: effects of probenecid and haloperidol, in Catecholamines: Basic and Clinical Frontiers, Vol 2. Edited by Usdin E, Kopin IJ, Barchas J. New York, Pergamon, 1979, pp 1887–1889

Kendler KS, Heninger GR, Roth RH: Brain contribution to the haloperidol-induced increase in plasma homovanillic acid. Eur J Pharmacol 71:321–326, 1981

Kendler KS, Heninger GR, Roth RH: Influence of dopamine agonists on plasma and brain levels of homovanillic acid. Life Sci 30:2063–2069, 1982

Kendler KS, Mohs RC, Davis KL: The effect of diet and physical activity on plasma homovanillic acid in normal human subjects. Psychiatry Res 8:215–224, 1983

Kopin IJ, Bankiewicz KS, Harvey-White J: Assessment of brain dopamine metabolism from plasma HVA and MHPG during debrisoquin treatment: validation in monkeys treated with MPTP. Neuropsychopharmacology 1:119–125, 1988

Maas JW, Hattox SE, Martin DM, et al: A direct method for determining dopamine synthesis and output of dopamine metabolites from brain in awake animals. J Neurochem 32:839–843, 1979a

Maas JW, Hattox SE, Greene NM, et al: 3-Methoxy-4-hydroxy-phenethyleneglycol production by human brain in vivo. Science 205:1025–1027, 1979b

Maas JW, Hattox SE, Greene NM, et al: Estimates of dopamine and serotonin synthesis by the awake human brain. J Neurochem 34:1547–1549, 1980a

Maas JW, Hattox SE, Landis DH: Variance in the production of homovanillic acid and 3-methoxy-4-hydroxyphenethyleneglycol by the awake primate brain. Life Sci 26:929–934, 1980b

Maas JW, Contreras SA, Seleshi E, et al: Dopamine metabolism and disposition in schizophrenic patients: studies using debrisoquin. Arch Gen Psychiatry 45:553–559, 1988

Mignot E, Garcia A, Laude D, et al: Value of plasma HVA level in human: influence of renal function, food intake, and psychiatric state. Biogenic Amines 5:169–176, 1988

Nedopil N, Pflieger R, Rüther E: The prediction of acute response, remission, and general outcome of neuroleptic treatment in acute schizophrenic patients. Pharmacopsychiatria 16:201–205, 1983

Pickar D: Perspectives on a time-dependent model of neuroleptic action. Schizophr Bull 14:255–268, 1988

Pickar D, Labarca R, Linnoila M, et al: Neuroleptic-induced decrease in plasma homovanillic acid and antipsychotic activity in schizophrenic patients. Science 225:954–957, 1984

Pickar D, Labarca R, Doran AR, et al: Longitudinal measurement of plasma homovanillic acid levels in schizophrenic patients. Arch Gen Psychiatry 43:669–676, 1986

Post RM, Goodwin FK: Time-dependent effects of phenothiazines on dopamine turnover in psychiatric patients. Science 190:488–499, 1975

Riddle MA, Leckman JF, Anderson GM, et al: Plasma free homovanillic acid: within-and across-day stability in children and adults with Tourette's syndrome. Life Sci 40:2145–2151, 1987

Scheinin H: Enhanced noradrenergic neuronal activity increases homovanillic acid in cerebrospinal fluid. J Neurochem 47:665–667, 1986

Scheinin M, Syvälahti EKG, Hietala J, et al: Effects of apomorphine on blood levels of HVA, growth hormone, and prolactin in medicated schizophrenics and healthy control subjects. Prog Neuropsychopharmacol Biol Psychiatry 9:441–449, 1985

Singh MM: Dysphoric response to neuroleptic treatment in schizophrenia and its prognostic significance. Diseases of the Nervous System 37:191–196, 1976

Sternberg DE, Bowers MB Jr, Heninger GR, et al: Lithium prevents adaptation of brain dopamine systems to haloperidol in schizophrenic patients. Psychiatry Res 10:79–86, 1983

Van Putten T, May PRA, Marder SR, et al: Subjective response to antipsychotic drugs. Arch Gen Psychiatry 38:187–190, 1981

Wolkowitz OM, Breier A, Doran A, et al: Alprazolam augmentation of the antipsychotic effects of fluphenazine in schizophrenic patients. Arch Gen Psychiatry 45:664–671, 1988

Chapter 3

Positron Emission Tomography in the Study of Neuroleptic Response

Adam Wolkin, M.D.

Chapter 3

Positron Emission Tomography in the Study of Neuroleptic Response

Positron emission tomography (PET) is a powerful and versatile technique that offers multiple windows for imaging of the brain. From the vantage point of the study of schizophrenia, the development of ligands that image dopamine receptor binding is of particular import.

Several groups have attempted to develop models that specifically derive estimates of dopamine receptor density using PET measures of dopamine ligand uptake (Farde et al. 1986; Wong et al. 1986a, 1986b). Obviously, this is critical to the fundamental question of the role of abnormal dopamine receptor density in schizophrenia. However, derivation of dopamine receptor B_{max} using PET is a complex and difficult problem, reflecting constraints imposed by human safety concerns (e.g., number of scans). As reviewed elsewhere (Swart and Korf 1987), each of the approaches to the quantitation of B_{max} has pragmatic and conceptual limitations.

A conservative approach that is a quantitative measure of binding, although not necessarily a direct expression of B_{max}, is the so-called ratio index method. As initially developed by Wong et al. (1984, 1986a) using the D_2 radioligand 11C-N-methylspiroperidol (NMS), the ratio index is based on the ratio of NMS uptake in striatum (representing total binding) as compared to cerebellum (representing nonspecific binding). Wong et al. have shown that this ratio is linear

The studies described here, conducted as part of the Brookhaven National Laboratory–New York University Medical Center PET program, were supported in part by the U.S. Department of Energy, the National Institutes of Health Grant NS-15638, NIMH MHCRC 30906, and the Veterans Administration. Haloperidol levels were determined by Tom Cooper at the Nathan Kline Institute, and the New York State Psychiatric Institute.

37

over time and an index of dopamine receptor binding. Limitations of this method—primarily the inordinate influence of blood flow during the relatively brief period of measurable uptake—have been obviated by the development of the longer-lived positron-emitting ligand 18F-NMS by the PET group at Brookhaven National Laboratory (Arnett et al. 1986). The ratio index using 18F-NMS has been shown to be linear with respect to time as well as stable for at least 4 hours (Smith et al. 1988).

As an index of receptor binding, the ratio index method using 18F-NMS is of particular value in measuring relative changes in dopamine receptor availability (or, conversely, occupancy) as a result of treatment with neuroleptics. This method may be employed to address several questions basic to the psychopharmacology of schizophrenia. In the remainder of this chapter, I will overview results of our PET studies to date with 18F-NMS in which we have begun to address some of these questions.

IN VIVO MEASURES OF DOPAMINE RECEPTOR BLOCKADE: THE MISSING LINK

One of the striking findings in psychopharmacology is the marked interindividual variation in neuroleptic metabolism, such that hundredfold differences in plasma level have been reported at the same dose (Curry and Marshall 1968; Curry et al. 1970). This variability in metabolism is thought to underlie the broad range of neuroleptic doses needed to effect therapeutic response in different patients. Recognition of the variability in drug metabolism has also led to an intense study of the relation between neuroleptic plasma levels and clinical effects to develop a more scientifically founded basis of neuroleptic treatment (Curry 1985).

An assumption implicit in this approach is that neuroleptic plasma levels are an accurate reflection of the extent of central nervous system dopamine blockade. Prior to the advent of PET, this assumption was untestable; direct measures of dopamine receptor blockade during neuroleptic treatment in human subjects were vital and missing data. Given the ability to measure dopamine blockade with PET, a basic question to be addressed first is whether there is, in fact, a relation between neuroleptic plasma level and dopamine receptor occupancy. Demonstration of such a relation would validate the continued use of plasma level in the study of neuroleptic effects, as well as augment the clinical utility of plasma levels as a rationale guide to neuroleptic treatment. (Ironically, it would also eventually obviate the need for PET in such studies.)

Another basic yet critical question of both research and clinical importance is the time necessary for neuroleptic washout. Measures of tissue neuroleptic concentrations in animals, as well as clinical experience, indicate that weeks to months may be necessary (Cohen et al. 1988). However, such studies do not necessarily assess the rate of change in actual receptor occupancy. Again, PET imaging of dopamine receptors offers a means to address this question directly.

Aside from these fundamental concerns, the most intriguing application of measurement of dopamine receptor blockade is in relation to clinical response. Among the questions awaiting study are 1) whether there is a minimal degree of receptor blockade necessary for antipsychotic efficacy, 2) whether there is a graded response with varying degrees of blockade, 3) whether neuroleptic treatment at particularly high doses actually results in an increase in receptor blockade, and 4) whether there are differences in levels of receptor blockade at which extrapyramidal side effects occur as opposed to therapeutic effects.

To date, these questions have been partially addressed using either dose or plasma level as an index of neuroleptic effect. One of the most controversial issues has been the relation between dose/plasma level and clinical response.

Early dose-response studies were subject to several methodological problems, including use of neuroleptic nonresponders, reliance on dose rather than plasma level, problems regarding measurement of plasma level, and use of variable rather than fixed doses. However, even in more recent studies where many of these concerns have been addressed, the data are still contradictory—for example, whether or not there is a therapeutic window for haloperidol (Volavka and Cooper 1987). Overall, most studies suggest that the optimal plasma level range for haloperidol is approximately 5–15 ng/ml (see references in Guthrie et al. 1987). PET measures of dopamine receptor occupancy offer a more theoretical underpinning to these empirical studies by linking plasma level to degree of receptor blockade in comparison to clinical response.

As noted above, other issues for which there exist largely empirical data include suggestions that currently promulgated neuroleptic regimens are excessive and that high doses produce no additional antipsychotic effect at the expense of increased psychotoxicity (Baldessarini et al. 1988). Again, demonstration of the relation between plasma level, receptor blockade, and both therapeutic effects and side effects would hopefully provide more direct answers to these questions.

Perhaps the area where the ability to measure receptor blockade directly has the most clinical significance is in the assessment of neuroleptic nonresponse. Based largely on the recognition of the variability in neuroleptic metabolism, nonresponse, at least in the clinical setting, is often suspected to reflect inadequate drug level. The consequence is increasingly larger neuroleptic doses (Jus et al. 1978). A key question is whether there is adequate dopamine blockade in nonresponders. With comparable treatment, less blockade in non-responders would suggest that pharmacokinetic differences underlie nonresponse (i.e., differences in drug metabolism or in crossing the blood-brain barrier). Conversely, comparable levels of blockade might suggest a more fundamental difference in the pathophysiology of schizophrenia.

Several investigators have attempted to unravel this question by studying the efficacy of neuroleptic megadoses in treatment-refractory patients, based on the rationale that such large doses would surmount pharmacokinetic barriers, if, indeed, this were the basis for nonresponse. Some studies in chronic patients hospitalized for long periods noted modest improvement after doses of fluphenazine of 800–1,200 mg/day (Klein et al. 1980 and references therein). However, a controlled study comparing doses of fluphenazine of 30 mg/day versus 1,200 mg/day in patients refractory to 6 weeks of standard treatment but who had not been hospitalized more than 2 months showed worsening of psychosis and akinesia in the megadose group, and continued improvement with additional time of treatment at traditional doses (Quitkin et al. 1975).

The perplexing problem of the basis for neuroleptic nonresponse may be more directly addressed using PET. In the sections that follow, I will present our findings regarding this and other questions raised above and discuss directions for future studies.

PLASMA LEVEL: DOPAMINE RECEPTOR OCCUPANCY RELATIONS

One of the basic prerequisite questions in studying neuroleptic effects is the time course of diminution in receptor occupancy after neuroleptic discontinuation. Using PET and 18F-NMS, we measured dopamine receptor occupancy at several time points prior to and subsequent to neuroleptic discontinuation in 16 schizophrenic patients (Smith et al. 1988). PET measures were obtained at baseline and after 12, 36, and 156 hours in one subgroup and at after 24 hours discontinuation in another subgroup of subjects.

As in all studies to be described, dopamine receptor binding of NMS was measured using a PETT VI instrument (Ter-Pogossian et al. 1982). Head positioning was established using localizing lasers for alignment and fitted foam headholders for stabilization. Approximately 5 mCi of 18F-NMS (specific activity range, 1–10 Ci/μmole) were injected over 10 seconds through an indwelling catheter. Counts were recorded in the high resolution mode (transverse resolution = 8 × 8 mm) over the next 3–4 hours, with four to seven scan epochs of up to 20 minutes. Regions of interest were visually identified in the striatum and cerebellum using computed tomography scans as additional reference for anatomic localization. The same coordinates were used in analyzing all scans. Receptor binding (i.e., availability) for NMS was estimated by the ratio index method (slope × 100) of striatal: cerebellar NMS uptake versus time. Uptake in both regions were determined as the decay-corrected regional activity concentrations for each scan epoch. The ratio index was determined as the slope of the regression line of the ratio striatal/cerebellar uptake on time.

Based on the ratio index values for NMS binding, there was a rapid and marked increase in dopamine receptor availability within days of neuroleptic discontinuation, reflecting decrease in dopamine receptor occupancy. Dopamine receptor availability doubled within the first 24 hours, with close to complete elimination of occupancy (based on comparison to uptake values in controls) within 1 week.

Similar data have been reported by Cambon et al. (1987) using 76Br-bromospiperone. This rate of decrease in dopamine receptor occupancy appears to be far more rapid than suggested by clinical experience, where relapse is usually measured in weeks to months after discontinuation, and by biochemical studies, where measurable neuroleptic or metabolite levels persist for months (Cohen et al. 1988; Johnson et al. 1967; Sakalis et al. 1972). It should be emphasized, however, that these PET data reflect only change in receptor occupancy. They do not necessarily reflect the physiologic sequelae of receptor blockade, such as change in dopamine system activity or dopamine receptor density. In this regard, there would appear to be a dissociation between the removal of dopamine receptor blockade itself and the clinical effects, paralleling the dissociation between the rapid onset of dopamine receptor blockade after drug initiation and the delay in onset of antipsychotic effects. From a practical standpoint, these data support the use of relatively short washouts, at least in PET studies of dopamine receptor occupancy.

Smith et al. (1988) also measured haloperidol levels concurrently with the PET scans to assess the relation between plasma level and receptor occupancy. There was a highly linear correlation between these two measures within this range of haloperidol plasma levels (<1–15 ng/cc). In a subsequent study (Wolkin et al. 1989b), we also obtained PET scans of NMS binding in 10 schizophrenic patients both during neuroleptic washout and again after several weeks treatment with haloperidol at plasma levels with a range of 10–90 ng/ml. Combining these data with the data Smith et al. provided, 26 subjects and 35 scans from which receptor blockade could be correlated with plasma haloperidol levels.

Together these points define a curvilinear relationship between plasma level and dopamine receptor occupancy (Figure 3-1). There are several salient features of this curve. There is very little scatter about the curve, implying a close relationship between plasma level and receptor occupancy over a wide plasma level range. This is strong support for the clinical utility of plasma neuroleptic levels as in index of central dopamine blockade. It remains for subsequent studies to quantify this relationship more precisely to develop predictive value of plasma levels.

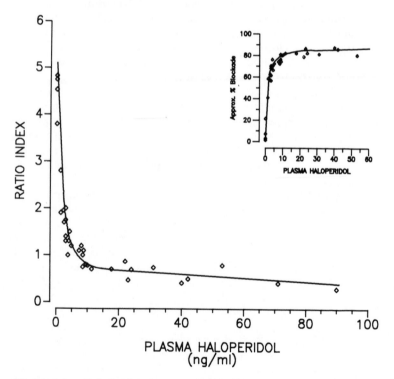

Figure 3-1. Relationship between plasma haloperidol level and receptor availability (ratio index), or approximate percentage of receptor blockade (*inset*).

There is a rapid and near linear increase in receptor occupancy at low plasma levels that tapers off at approximately 5–15 ng/ml. This direct and independent observation is remarkably congruent with clinical studies showing this to be the initial phase of therapeutic levels for haloperidol (Guthrie et al. 1987).

Above 20 ng/ml, there is an asymptotic relation between plasma level and receptor blockade, with relatively little additional increase in receptor blockade even with marked increase in plasma levels. This is consistent with the growing clinical consensus that there is little added benefit of treatment with high or megadose haloperidol treatment (Baldessarini et al. 1988) specifically corresponding to plasma levels above 20 ng/ml. This is not to suggest that there may not be some patients who benefit from higher doses; this would be expected in those patients who, in fact, have abnormalities in neuroleptic metabolism. Nor does it rule out the possibility that there may be a small subgroup of schizophrenic patients where, for purposes of illustration, 95% receptor blockade is efficacious as compared to 90%.

NEUROLEPTIC RESPONSE: DOPAMINE RECEPTOR OCCUPANCY RELATIONS

The data from the studies above characterize the relation between receptor blockade and neuroleptic plasma levels, supporting the clinical utility of the latter, but do not address the relation between receptor blockade and actual response. To begin to assess if there are differences in degree of receptor blockade between neuroleptic responders and nonresponders, we measured NMS binding before and after haloperidol treatment in these two groups (Wolkin et al. 1989a). The study was based on the premise that a difference in receptor blockade would imply pharmacokinetic factors or central nervous system penetration as the basis of treatment nonresponse, whereas comparable values would suggest that neuroleptic non-response cannot simply be attributed to inadequate receptor block-ade. The results would also indicate the percentage of change in receptor blockade associated with antipsychotic efficacy (at least in this sample).

Subjects included 10 schizophrenic inpatients ages 18–49 years. Following at least a 9-day neuroleptic washout, subjects underwent baseline ratings and PET 18F-NMS scan. They were then started on haloperidol. The dose was titrated according to clinical response up to a maximum plasma level of at least 10 ng/ml. Patients were carefully observed for side effects, which were controlled by either dose reduction or treatment with anticholinergics. The rationale for the variable dose schedule was to afford each patient an optimal chance for response, at least in terms of maximally tolerated neuroleptic level.

Subjects underwent a repeat PET scan and concurrent psychiatric ratings 4–6 weeks after initiation of haloperidol and after at least 1 week on a fixed dose. Haloperidol levels were also obtained at this time for later analysis using a modification of a GLC method (Bianchetti and Morselli 1978).

Subjects were classified as responders or nonresponders based on a criterion of lack of efficacy as less than a 20% decrease in total Brief Psychiatric Rating Scale (BPRS) total score (Overall and Gorham 1962). Five subjects were thus classified as nonresponders; the other five subjects showed robust antipsychotic effects (mean decreases in BPRS total score for the two groups were 4% and 40%, respectively). Nonresponders had prominent positive symptoms that could be expected to respond to neuroleptics, and that were comparable in severity to those in responders (mean ± SD BPRS total scores and positive symptom scores derived from the BPRS were 35 ± 4 and 22 ± 2 for responders and 42 ± 5 and 27 ± 4 for nonresponders). Mean haloperidol levels for responders and nonresponders were 32 (range, 22–42 ng/ml) and 50 (range 10–90 ng/ml), respectively.

The results of the PET scans are shown in Figure 3-2. The changes in NMS binding after neuroleptic treatment were virtually identical for responders and nonresponders, indicating comparable levels of dopamine receptor blockade by haloperidol. On average, both groups had marked decreases in measurable dopamine receptor availability, as indicated by actual posttreatment slope values (ratio index/100) of less than 0.006. (The complete absence of any specific binding to striatum would theoretically result in a slope of zero.)

Further, across the entire range of plasma levels among nonresponders, blockade in nonresponders was equal to or greater than that in responders with similar plasma levels. These data are direct evidence that neuroleptic nonresponse may not necessarily be due to inadequate neuroleptic blockade. The almost identical means for both groups imply that there may be a marked overlap in general between responders and nonresponders in extent of neuroleptic blockade.

Therapeutic doses of haloperidol resulted in 85% or greater average decreases in receptor availability. These results are consistent with PET data from other groups (Farde et al. 1986, 1988; Wong et al. 1985, 1986b). Unanswered, as yet, is the minimum percentage of change in receptor binding associated with antipsychotic efficacy. This would be of marked value, in conjunction with a well-characterized relation between occupancy and plasma level, in directly ascertaining the plasma level threshold needed for response. Although the above data suggest an approximate plasma level range where this may occur, future plasma level ranging studies are needed to answer this question.

Also unanswered are several other key questions noted earlier: whether response is all or none at a given threshold or increases within a plasma level range, and the relation between occupancy and the onset of therapeutic effects versus side effects. Again, these questions will necessitate dose-ranging PET studies in a larger number of subjects.

Perhaps most perplexing is the lack of response in the face of "therapeutic" levels of dopamine receptor blockade. In broadest terms, this observation suggests there may be differences in the biology of schizophrenia in nonresponders. For example, there may be a subgroup of schizophrenic patients or a stage of the illness where dopaminergic activity is not critical to the pathophysiology. This hypothesis should be addressed in future studies by comparison of

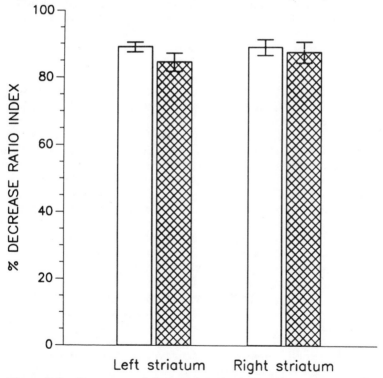

Figure 3-2. Percentage of decrease in striatal dopamine receptor availability (as measured by the ratio index method) after treatment with haloperidol for responders (*open bars*) and nonresponders (*cross-hatched bars*).

clinical response, PET measures of receptor occupancy, and biochemical measures of dopamine system activity.

Alternatively, nonresponse might also reflect a concomitant abnormality in the regulation of dopaminergic activity, such that it is not sufficiently diminished by neuroleptics. What this abnormality might entail is speculative at present. However, the dissociation between onset or loss of therapeutic response and initiation/discontinuation of receptor blockade supports the notion that there are time-dependent changes in dopamine activity as a consequence of receptor blockade that may be critical to clinical efficacy.

Based on their electrophysiologic studies in animals, Bunney and Grace (1978) and White and Wang (1982) have suggested that this mechanism entails a gradual decrease in presynaptic dopamine activity through depolarization blockade of the dopamine neuron. They hypothesized that postsynaptic dopamine blockade is inadequate to overcome neuroleptic-induced adaptive changes in dopamine release; it is only the eventual concomitant decrease in presynaptic release that sufficiently reduces dopamine activity. Several studies suggest that depolarization blockade is mediated either through postsynaptic neuronal feedback loops (Bunney and Grace 1978; White and Wang 1982) or by autoreceptor regulation of presynaptic activity (Chiodo and Bunney 1983). Abnormalities in these regulatory systems might conceivably account for neuroleptic nonresponse in the face of robust receptor blockade.

Consistent with this hypothesis are biochemical measures of dopamine turnover during neuroleptic treatment. Several investigators have reported that neuroleptic treatment is associated with a gradual decline in homovanillic acid when followed for several weeks (Bowers et al. 1986; Davidson et al. 1987; Pickar et al. 1984, 1986). Most fascinating are the reports of Bowers et al. (1984) and Pickar et al. (1984, 1986) that the magnitude of decrease correlates with the extent of clinical improvement; and that following neuroleptic discontinuation, there is a comparable relation between increase in homovanillic acid and symptom exacerbation.

In contrast to some of the other questions reviewed here, it is unclear how imaging of dopamine receptors may be further applied to study the mechanisms underlying nonresponse if the "defect" is not at the level of receptor occupancy. The challenge to PET research in this regard will be to develop methods to assess the functional effects of dopamine system activity, as opposed to static measures of receptor occupancy. Potential methods might include measure of glucose utilization, assuming that the downstream effects of dopamine activity are more focal than presently suggested (Wolkin et al. 1987), or development of other neurochemical probes that would assess secondary effects of dopamine receptor blockade, including dopamine turnover.

REFERENCES

Arnett CD, Wolf AP, Shiue C-Y, et al: Improved delineation of human dopamine receptors using [18F]-N-methylspiroperidol and PET. J Nucl Med 27: 1878–1882, 1986

Baldessarini R, Cohen BM, Teicher MH: Significance of neuroleptic dose and plasma level in the pharmacological treatment of psychoses. Arch Gen Psychiatry 45:79–91, 1988

Bianchetti G, Morselli PL: Rapid and sensitive method for determination of haloperidol in human samples using nitrogen-phosphorus selective detection. J Chromatogr 153: 203–209, 1978

Bowers MB Jr, Swigar ME, Jatlow PI, et al: Plasma catecholamine metabolites and early response to haloperidol. J Clin Psychiatry 45:249–251, 1984

Bowers MB Jr, Swigar ME, Jatlow PI, et al: Early neuroleptic response in psychotic men and women: correlation with plasma HVA and MHPG. Compr Psychiatry 27:181–185, 1986

Bunney BS, Grace AA: Acute and chronic haloperidol treatment: comparison of effects on nigral dopaminergic cell activity. Life Sci 23:1715–1728, 1978

Cambon H, Baron JC, Boulenger JP, et al: In vivo assay for neuroleptic receptor binding in the striatum. Br J Psychiatry 151:824–830, 1987

Chiodo LA, Bunney BS: Typical and atypical neuroleptics: differential effects of chronic administration on the activity of A9 and A10 midbrain dopaminergic neurons. J Neurosci 3:1607–1619, 1983

Cohen BM, Barb S, Campbell A, et al: Persistence of haloperidol in the brain. Arch Gen Psychiatry 45:879–880, 1988

Curry SH: Commentary: the strategy and value of neuroleptic drug monitoring. J Clin Psychopharmacol 5:263–271, 1985

Curry SH, Marshall JHL: Plasma levels of chlorpromazine and some of its relatively nonpolar metabolites in psychiatric patients. Life Sci 7:9–17, 1968

Curry SH, Davis JM, Janowsky DS, et al: Factors affecting chlorpromazine levels in psychiatric patients. Arch Gen Psychiatry 3:209–215, 1970

Davidson M, Losonczy MF, Mohs RC, et al: Effects of debrisoquin and haloperidol on plasma homovanillic acid concentration in schizophrenic patients. Neuropsychopharmacology 1:17–23, 1987

Farde L, Hall H, Ehrin E, et al: Quantitative analysis of D2 dopamine receptor binding in the living human brain by PET. Science 231:258–261, 1986

Farde L, Wiesel W, Halldin C, et al: Central D2-dopamine receptor occupancy in schizophrenic patients treated with antipsychotic drugs. Arch Gen Psychiatry 45:71–76, 1988

Guthrie S, Lane EA, Linnoila M: Monitoring of plasma drug concentrations in clinical psychopharmacology, in Psychopharmacology: The Third Generation of Progress. Edited by Meltzer HY. New York, Raven, 1987, pp 1323–1338

Johnson PC, Charalampous KD, Braun GA: Absorption and excretion of tritiated haloperidol in man: a preliminary report. International Journal of Neuropsychiatry 3 (suppl 1): 524–525, 1967

Jus A, Villeneuve A, Jus K: Therapeutic dilemma in neuroleptic-resistant psychotic disorders, in Neuropsychopharmacology, Vol 1. Edited by Deniker P, Radouco-Thomas C, Villeneuve A. Oxford, Pergamon, 1978, pp 331–338

Klein DF, Gittelman R, Quitkin F, et al: Diagnosis and Drug Treatment of Psychiatric Disorders: Adults and Children, 2nd Edition. Baltimore, MD, Williams & Wilkins, 1980

Overall JE, Gorham DR: The Brief Psychiatric Rating Scale. Psychol Rep 10:799–812, 1962

Pickar D, Labarca R, Linnoila M, et al: Neuroleptic-induced decrease in plasma homovanillic acid and antipsychotic activity in schizophrenic patients. Science 225:954–957, 1984

Pickar D, Labarca R, Doran AB, et al: Longitudinal measurement of plasma homovanillic acid levels in schizophrenic patients. Arch Gen Psychiatry 43:669–676, 1986

Quitkin F, Rifkin A, Klein DF: A double blind study of very high dosage versus standard dosage fluphenazine in nonchronic treatment refractory schizophrenia. Arch Gen Psychiatry 32:1276–1281, 1975

Sakalis G, Curry SH, Mould GP, et al: Physiological and clinical effects of chlorpromazine and their relationship to plasma level. Clin Pharmacol Ther 13:931–946, 1972

Smith M, Wolf AP, Brodie JD, et al: Serial [18F]-N-methylspiroperidol PET studies to measure change in antipsychotic drug D2 receptor occupancy in schizophrenic patients. Biol Psychiatry 23:653–663, 1988

Swart JAA, Korf J: In vivo dopamine receptor assessment for clinical studies using positron emission tomography. Biochem Pharmacol 36:2241–2250, 1987

Ter-Pogossian MM, Ficke DC, Hood JT, et al: PETT VI: a positron emission tomography utilizing cesium fluoride scintillation detectors. J Comp Assist Tomogr 6:125, 1982

Volavka J, Cooper TB: Review of haloperidol blood level and clinical response: looking through the window. J Clin Psychopharmacol 7:25–30, 1987

White FJ, Wang RY: Comparison of the effects of chronic haloperidol treatment on A9 and A10 dopamine neurons in the rat. Life Sci 32:983–993, 1982

Wolkin A, Angrist B, Wolf A, et al: Effects of amphetamine on local cerebral metabolism in normal and schizophrenic subjects as determined by positron emission tomography. Psychopharmacology 92:241–246, 1987

Wolkin A, Barouche F, Wolf AP, et al: Dopamine blockade and clinical response: evidence for two biological subgroups of schizophrenia. Am J Psychiatry 146:905–908, 1989a

Wolkin A, Brodie JD, Barouche F, et al: Dopamine receptor occupancy and plasma haloperidol levels. Arch Gen Psychiatry 46:482–483, 1989b

Wong DF, Wagner HN, Dannals RF, et al: Effects of age on dopamine and serotonin receptors measured by positron tomography in the living human brain. Science 226:1393–1396, 1984

Wong DF, Wagner HN, Coyle J, et al: Assessment of dopamine receptor blockade by neuroleptic drugs in the living human brain. J Nucl Med 26:52, 1985

Wong DF, Gjedde A, Wagner HN: Quantification of neuroreceptors in the living human brain, I: irreversible binding of ligands. J Cereb Blood Flow Metab 6:137–146, 1986a

Wong DF, Gjedde A, Wagner HN, et al: Quantification of neuroreceptors in the living human brain, II: inhibition studies of receptor density and affinity. J Cereb Blood Flow Metab 6:147–153, 1986b

Chapter 4

Schizophrenia: Alternative Neuroleptic Strategies

Celeste A. Johns, M.D.
David I. Mayerhoff, M.D.
Jeffrey A. Lieberman, M.D.
John M. Kane, M.D.

Chapter 4

Schizophrenia: Alternative Neuroleptic Strategies

Antipsychotic medications are the mainstay of the pharmacologic treatment of schizophrenia. Numerous placebo-controlled studies have established the efficacy of neuroleptics in the acute treatment of psychotic symptoms, with symptom relief typically occurring within 4–6 weeks of initiation of treatment (Cole et al. 1966). It is recognized, however, that a substantial proportion of acutely exacerbated schizophrenic patients do not have a satisfactory response to an initial course of antipsychotic medication. The treatment of such patients is a major concern of clinicians. This issue is made even more critical by increasing pressure to shorten the length of hospital stays. Many clinicians feel pressured to alter the pharmacologic treatment plan after 1–2 weeks of treatment if substantial improvement has not occurred. This may result in patients receiving unnecessarily high doses or being prematurely switched to different medications. At present, these decisions are not based on evidence from systematic, well-controlled trials. The current body of knowledge about some of the factors that may impact on initial treatment response, including drug dosage, drug blood level, drug type, and duration of administration, will be reviewed so that current clinical practices and future research directions may be clarified.

In reviewing a large series of acute treatment studies providing data on dosage and response, Davis et al. (1980) suggested that the optimal dosage for the average patient undergoing treatment for an acute exacerbation of a schizophrenic disorder is approximately 500–1,000 mg of chlorpromazine (or equivalent) per day. It is clear from our understanding of drug absorption and metabolism (Kane 1987; Kane et al. 1976) that there are considerable individual differences in drug blood levels achieved after the ingestion of the same oral dosage. It is possible that some patients receiving a presumably adequate oral dosage of a given antipsychotic drug may not have sufficient circulating active drug reaching the target site to produce a clinical response.

In such patients, raising the dosage beyond that usually given might produce a better clinical response.

Consideration of drug dosage leads to questions about the relationship between drug dose, neuroleptic blood level, and clinical response. While there is a growing body of literature on this subject, much of it suffers from a variety of methodological problems, which have limited the conclusions that can be drawn in this area. Specifically, many such studies have involved a relatively short duration of treatment, which would not allow for the possibility that antipsychotic response may occur in stages with some variability in time course across symptoms. In addition, many studies have not maintained appropriate control groups. In any study in which a manipulation of drug blood levels is thought to be responsible for subsequent improvement, a control group of patients maintained on the original blood level for an equal duration as that following blood level manipulation is essential. Without such a control group, it cannot be ascertained positively whether improvement is due to the dosage manipulation or to the increased length of time for which the patient is receiving the antipsychotic medication. Yet other studies that demonstrated a correlation between low drug blood levels and clinical nonresponse did not increase drug dose in a subgroup of nonresponders to assess whether increasing neuroleptic blood levels would enhance clinical response. A case in point is the study by Smith et al. (1979), in which a group of chronic, nonresponding schizophrenic patients were compared with treatment-responsive schizophrenics. On the same medication regimen, blood levels of butaperazine were lower in both plasma and red blood cells after single and chronic dosing in the nonresponders. These results might suggest that low blood levels of neuroleptics may be one important factor in the poor clinical response of schizophrenic patients who are classified as "drug-refractory" patients. Unfortunately, this investigation did not carry out the next logical step, which would be to increase the dosage of antipsychotic medication in a controlled design in those refractory patients with low neuroleptic blood levels.

A possible curvilinear relationship between blood (and in some reports, red blood cell) neuroleptic levels has been hypothesized and examined extensively in the recent literature. Results of 18 studies involving some type of fixed-dose design are summarized in Table 4-1. Reports focusing on treatment-resistant patients have been excluded, because such studies would not be expected to produce results that would be generalizable to the population of acutely exacerbated schizophrenic patients with whom this review is concerned. Exclusion of studies that do not use a fixed-dose design is

Table 4-1. Neuroleptic blood levels and clinical response

Reference	N	Dose	Duration (days)	Method	Blood level (ng/ml)	Results	Window (ng/ml)
Smith et al. (1984)	26	Thioridazine, fixed-random	24	GLC	195–1685 (thioridazine & mesoridazine)	No significant correlation	No
Wode-Helgodt et al. (1978)	38	Chlorpromazine, fixed-random	28	GC/MS	0–150	Significant correlation at 2 but not 4 weeks	No
Dysken et al. (1981)	29	Fluphenazine, fixed	15	GLC	.1–4.4	Significant correlation	Yes .2–2.28
Cohen et al. (1980b)	11	Thioridazine, fixed	14	RRA	1,100–6,200	Significant correlation	No
Bergling et al. (1975)	40	Thioridazine or thiothixene	56	Fluorometric	Thioridazine 1,000–6,000; thiothixene 0–160	No significant correlation	No
Neborsky et al. (1984)	20	Haloperidol, fixed-random	7	RIA	Low dose (2 dosage groups) $\bar{X} = 8.2$ High dose $\bar{X} = 34.0$	Plasma: RBC correlation with response	No
Garver et al. (1977)	10	Butaperazine, flexible-fixed	12	Fluorometric	2.3–321	Plasma & RBC curvilinear relationship	30–80 RBC
Garver et al. (1984)	14	Haloperidol, fixed-random	17	GLC	.7–87	Significant correlation for plasma but not RBC	Window for plasma but not RBC
Smith et al. (1985)	33	Haloperidol, fixed-random	24	GLC	2–23	Significant correlation	Plasma: 6.5–16.5; RBC: 2.2–6.8

Table 4-1. Neuroleptic blood levels and clinical response (continued)

Reference	N	Dose	Duration (days)	Method	Blood level (ng/ml)	Results	Window (ng/ml)
Mavroidis et al. (1983)	14	Haloperidol, fixed-random	14	GLC	2–19	Significant correlation	Plasma: 4.2–11.0
Mavroidis et al. (1984)	19	Fluphenazine, fixed-random	14	GC	.1–2.4	Significant correlation	Plasma: .1–.7; RBC: .2–.6
Cohen et al. (1980a)	58	Various drugs, flexible-partial fixed	?	RRA	—	Significant correlation	No
Casper et al. (1980)	24	Butaperazine, random-fixed	14	Fluorometric	23–250	Significant correlation with RBC, but not plasma	RBC only: 30–60
Potkin et al. (1985)	73	Haloperidol, flexible-fixed	42	RIA	0–75	Trend	Curviliner (trend) 4–26
Van Putten et al. (1985)	47	Haloperidol, random-fixed	28	RIA	?	Significant at 1 but not 2 or 4 weeks	Curvilinear at 1 week (5–16) but no relationship at 2 or 4 weeks
Magliozzi et al. (1981)	17	Haloperidol, flexible-fixed	21–84	GLC	0–96	Significant correlation	8–17.7
Bolvig-Hansen et al. (1981)	14	Perphenazine, flexible-fixed	56	GC	.6–10.1	No significant correlation	No
May et al. (1981)	48	Chlorpromazine, fixed	28	GC/MS	?	No significant correlation (plasma or saliva)	No

Note. GLC = gas liquid chromatography, GC/MS = gas chromatography/mass spectroscopy, RRA = radioreceptor assay, RIA = radioimmunoassay, RBC = red blood cell.
Source. Modified from Kane 1987.

essential; the alternative, in which dosage is adjusted based on clinical response, leads to selective increases in drug dosage (and, presumably, in neuroleptic blood level) in those patients who are intrinsically poor responders to neuroleptics regardless of dosage or blood level. Such studies might then conclude that blood neuroleptic levels are not correlated with response, or that high blood levels are counter-therapeutic. Many of the studies that do include a fixed-dose design have not utilized a high enough dose or a sample size large enough to define the upper limit of a putative therapeutic window. Despite these methodological limitations, half of the studies summarized in Table 4-1 do support a curvilinear relationship between drug blood levels and clinical response; several others found there to be a direct correlation between blood level and response rather than a "window." Thus an area of great importance for future research would be the exploration of the putative upper end of the dosage range to establish whether, in fact, clinical response maximizes and then stabilizes at higher blood neuroleptic levels or whether it begins to deteriorate beyond a certain point, as the window concept suggests.

High-dose or megadose neuroleptic treatment has been utilized experimentally in populations of refractory patients, but not yet in patients who have been selected on the basis of low neuroleptic blood levels. No consistent advantage has been demonstrated for higher than standard dosages (Bjorndal et al. 1980; Itil et al. 1970; Mc-Creadie and McDonald 1977; Morselli et al. 1980; Quitkin et al. 1975; Rimon et al. 1981).

High initial doses of neuroleptics, or "rapid neuroleptization," has not increased overall response rate nor has it significantly shortened response time (Donlon et al. 1980; Ericksen et al. 1978; Neborsky et al. 1981). It is our impression that such a strategy exposes the majority of patients to higher than necessary doses. Van Putten and Marder (1986) pioneered the hypothesis that very low doses, in fact, are effective for most acutely exacerbated schizophrenic inpatients. In addition, although the rate of improvement might be slower, the end points achieved utilizing doses of haloperidol and fluphenazine as low as 5 mg are the same as when 20 mg are given, with the low-dose group experiencing far fewer side effects. McEvoy et al. (1986) have begun to test the neuroleptic-threshold hypothesis in a systematic fashion. Their open pilot study suggested that a significant percentage of patients will improve on a very low dose of haloperidol. Haase (1961) further explored this low-dose concept by utilizing the first appearance of adverse effects of neuroleptics, specifically hypokinesia and rigidity, as a guide to identify sufficient and appropriate therapeutic doses of neuroleptics.

Another consideration in explaining the lack of response among some acutely exacerbated patients is that individuals may differ in their response to specific antipsychotic agents. The preclinical observation that antipsychotic drugs vary considerably in their relative affinities for specific brain receptors, including the dopamine receptor (which is suggested to mediate therapeutic response) (Hyttel et al. 1985; Richelson 1984), also supports the possibility that different drugs may have different spectrums of activity. On the other hand, it has been suggested that the milligram potency of various antipsychotic drugs does correlate with receptor affinity in theoretically relevant binding assays (Creese et al. 1976). On a clinical level, there is certainly some feeling, based largely on anecdotal evidence, that some patients do better on one drug than another. It is even widely taught that a patient's prior response to particular neuroleptics or a family history of response should guide the clinician's choice of antipsychotic medication for that patient. However, large pooled comparisons have consistently failed to show that any one antipsychotic drug is consistently superior to another, excluding perhaps the novel neuroleptic clozapine, which is beyond the scope of this review. Remarkably, there are very few reports in the literature that address this issue in a systematic fashion. Gardos (1974) switched stable schizophrenic patients who were undergoing maintenance treatment with "doctors' choice" antipsychotic medication to an alternative drug, double-blind, while some patients continued on their original medication, also double-blind. A significant increase in relapse rate among those switched suggested that the antipsychotic drugs were not interchangeable. It is difficult to confirm this, however, since dosage equivalencies of the major antipsychotic drugs are still not well established. In the Gardos study, therefore, patients whose medications were switched may have deteriorated based solely on an alteration of the absolute drug dosage. It should also be emphasized that this study did not address the issue of specificity of neuroleptic response in an acutely exacerbated schizophrenic population. It is still possible that switching medications in an acutely ill patient who is not responding to the first antipsychotic administered will improve the clinical response. It is critical in doing such a study to have a control group of patients who remain on the original treatment for an equal duration to control for the effect of additional time.

It is clear that, in the field at this time, the two standard alternative strategies for treating initial nonresponders are either to increase the dosage substantially or to switch to another antipsychotic drug. It is also apparent from reviewing the literature that some patients who do not demonstrate full response to an antipsychotic drug during the first 3–4 weeks of treatment may yet improve with the passage of additional time, *without* altering the treatment regimen. This further response has been apparent even in some studies of more refractory patients (Bjorndal et al. 1980; Itil et al. 1970; McCreadie and McDonald 1977; Quitkin et al. 1975), as illustrated by Table 4-2. In these four studies, refractory patients were randomly assigned to a standard dose or a high-dose treatment. None of these studies found a significant advantage for the higher dose, but it is of considerable interest to note the overall improvement rate in both treatment cells combined among these apparent neuroleptic nonresponders. This suggests that additional time on medication may lead to improvement even in this difficult-to-treat subgroup of patients. It is also possible that nonpharmacologic aspects of this research may have contributed to clinical improvement. In either case, these findings argue for the avoidance of premature closure and the need for systematic research with appropriate controls.

To summarize, when a patient who is not treatment refractory by history is admitted to a hospital for an acute exacerbation of a schizophrenic illness, a neuroleptic will almost invariably be given as a first-line treatment. If this patient has a less than optimal response after several weeks of this treatment trial, the literature suggests a number of possible alternative strategies. One might reasonably choose to increase the dose of the original neuroleptic, or to switch to a second neuroleptic, or to continue the same neuroleptic at the same dose for a greater period of time. Based on the work of McEvoy et al. (1986) and of Van Putten and Marder (1986), one might even

Table 4-2. Therapeutic response in neuroleptic-resistant schizophrenia

| | | | Overall improvement: combined groups | |
Reference	Drug(s)	Dosage (mg)	*n*	%
Itil et al. (1970)	Fluphenazine Fluphenazine	30 } 300 }	9/17	53
McCreadie and McDonald (1977)	Haloperidol Chlorpromazine	100 } 600 }	7/20	35
Quitkin et al. (1975)	Fluphenazine Fluphenazine	30 } 1,200 }	13/31	42
Bjorndal et al. (1980)	Haloperidol Haloperidol	15[a] } 103[a] }	10/23	43

[a]Mean.

choose to lower the dose of neuroleptic being prescribed. All of the above does not, of course, preclude the utility of various nonpharmacologic adjunctive strategies, which may also impact upon response; they have been omitted from this review as we are focusing solely on the issue of optimizing neuroleptic efficacy.

We are currently in the second year of a 5-year study designed to compare the relative efficacy and adverse effects of three alternative strategies for DSM-III-R (American Psychiatric Association 1987) diagnosed schizophrenic patients who fail to meet a priori criteria for improvement following a 4-week course of a standard treatment, which we have selected to be fluphenazine HCl 20 mg/day. Our definition of treatment response, chosen before the study began, is intended to be relevant and generalizable to common clinical practice. Responders must have no rating above 3 on any of the four Brief Psychiatric Rating Scale (BPRS) (Overall and Gorham 1962) items that specifically assess psychosis (conceptual disorganization, suspiciousness, hallucinations, and unusual thoughts), and also have a rating of 2 ("much improved") on the Clinical Global Impression (CGI) (Connors and Barkley 1985). A rating of 3 on the above BPRS items represents mild psychotic symptoms that usually do not interfere significantly with function; it is often unreasonable to expect further improvement, or the complete amelioration of psychotic symptoms, in a population of chronic schizophrenic patients.

Nonresponders will be randomly assigned double-blind to one of the following three experimental treatment groups: 1) continued treatment with fluphenazine HCl 20 mg/day for an additional 4 weeks; 2) increased dosage of fluphenazine HCl 80 mg/day for 4 weeks; or 3) switch to haloperidol 20 mg/day for 4 weeks (see Figure 4-1). Patients will be rated weekly to assess response, side effects, and the patients' subjective responses to the medication. In addition, plasma neuroleptic levels will be determined at fixed intervals during both phases of treatment to assess the relationship between neuroleptic blood level and clinical response.

This study, with three treatment cells, will require that a substantial number of subjects be studied. We anticipate that 40 patients will be treated in each cell, for a total of 120, in order to make our results valid and generalizable. For this reason, we have omitted other possible strategies, such as dosage reduction or the addition of ancillary medications, which would require yet a larger group of subjects. We have chosen fluphenazine HCl 20 mg/day as our initial, standard treatment, because this represents a dosage well within the range considered to be effective for the "average" patient.

The optimal treatment of acutely exacerbated schizophrenic

patients who are partially or completely refractory to the initial few weeks of neuroleptic therapy is one of the most common issues encountered by inpatient clinicians. Lack of systematic exploration of alternative treatment strategies has led to the implementation of multiple idiosyncratic treatment options based largely on anecdotal evidence or institutional tradition. We have undertaken a study of three of the more reasonable treatment strategies: 1) to raise the neuroleptic dosage, 2) to change the class of neuroleptic, or 3) to maintain a constant drug and dose over a longer period of time. At the conclusion of this study, we hope to have a well-researched body of data that can suggest future directions for further research as well as guidelines for optimal clinical management of the schizophrenic inpatient.

PRELIMINARY DATA

Pilot data and early study results are available for review at this time. As these data represent only 18 months of subject entry into a study that is projected to last 5 years, these results must be regarded as being very preliminary, and no valid conclusions can yet be drawn. The data gathered thus far, however, do pose intriguing questions about the time course and overall response rate of schizophrenic patients to neuroleptics. Of the first 38 subjects entered into the open fluphenazine treatment phase, 11 responded well according to our a priori criteria. Nine patients dropped out of this phase. Of the remaining 18 who completed phase 1 and were rated as non-

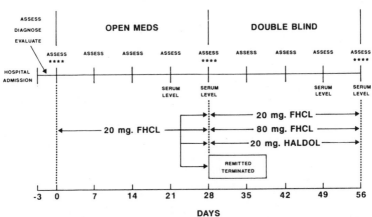

Figure 4-1. Study design. FHCL = fluphenazine HCL; HALDOL = haloperidol.

responders, 13 continued into the double-blind treatment (phase 2) (see Table 4-3).

Examination of the 29 subjects who completed the initial 4-week course of fluphenazine 20 mg/day reveals a response rate of only 37%, which seems surprisingly low. However, review of an earlier pilot study undertaken with 31 schizophrenic inpatients at our institution revealed an almost identical response rate (35%) to the same treatment condition. When entry and week 4 clinical ratings were compared for responders versus nonresponders, responders began the study with a mean CGI score of 4.9 and ended with a mean score of 2.7, versus means of 5.1 and 4.6, respectively, for the nonresponders. Thus the data do not suggest that our poor response rate is merely an artifact of a priori response criteria that are too strict to pick up all but the most dramatic clinical responders; rather, this cross-section of acutely ill newly hospitalized schizophrenic patients seems as a whole to respond poorly to this initial brief neuroleptic treatment. Responders did not differ from nonresponders in sex, age, week 4 serum fluphenazine levels, or even side effects; a majority of subjects experienced some degree of extrapyramidal side effects and equal numbers in each group reported akathisia.

Only 13 subjects entered the double-blind phase 2 at the time of this analysis, making interpretation of these results highly speculative (Table 4-4). On the whole, these initially nonresponsive patients continued to do poorly regardless of the treatment cell to which they

Table 4-3.   Phase 1: fluphenazine 20 mg

Responders	11
Nonresponders	
Entered phase 2	13
Not entered in phase 2	5
Dropouts	9
Total	38

Table 4-4.   Phase 2

Drug	Dosage (mg)	Nonresponder	Responder
Fluphenazine	20	5	0
Fluphenazine	80	3	1
Haloperidol	20	2	1

Note.   There was one dropout (fluphenazine 80 mg).

were assigned. Only two subjects responded to the additional 4 weeks of treatment, regardless of drug condition (one to fluphenazine 80 mg/day and one to haloperidol 20 mg/day). CGI ratings, which began at a mean of 4.6 at the initiation of double-blind treatment, fell only to 4.4 for the group as a whole at the conclusion of this treatment phase, which represents an insignificant change in clinical condition.

Review of our earlier pilot data again supports the generalizability of these results to a larger patient sample: 13 initially nonresponsive subjects entered various neuroleptic treatment cells in a study design similar to that currently in progress. Just as in our current sample, only two subjects met a priori response criteria for improvement after the additional 4 weeks of treatment.

The most striking feature of these preliminary data is the poor response of acutely exacerbated, hospitalized chronic schizophrenic patients to a standard course of treatment with neuroleptics. Only one-third of such patients responded well to an initial 4-week course of neuroleptic treatment; continued neuroleptic treatment for an additional 4 weeks, regardless of whether the neuroleptic class or dose was changed or held steady, resulted in almost no further improvement in clinical condition. Clearly, a much larger patient population must be studied before any firm conclusions can be reached. The small sample size presented here can provide us with speculative results at best. Documentation of rates of response as well as optimal neuroleptic management will provide guidelines to maximize response and minimize unnecessary neuroleptic-induced morbidity and may suggest future areas of investigation into more efficacious short- and long-term pharmacotherapy.

REFERENCES

American Psychiatric Association: Diagnostic and Statistical Manual of Mental Disorders, 3rd Edition, Revised. Washington, DC, American Psychiatric Association, 1987

Bergling R, Bjorndal T, Oreland L, et al: Plasma levels and clinical effects of thioridazine and thiothixene. J Clin Psychopharmacol 15:178–186, 1975

Bjorndal N, Bjerre M, Gerlach J, et al: High dosage haloperidol therapy in chronic schizophrenic patients: a double-blind study of clinical response, side effects, serum haloperidol and serum prolactin. Psychopharmacology 67:17–23, 1980

Bolvig-Hansen L, Larsen NE, Vestergard P: Plasma levels of perphenazine

(Trilafon) related to development of extrapyramidal side effects. Psychopharmacology 74:306–309, 1981

Casper R, Garver DL, Dekirmenjian H, et al: Phenothiazine levels in plasma and red blood cells: their relationship to clinical improvement in schizophrenia. Arch Gen Psychiatry 37:301–305, 1980

Cohen BM, Lipinski JF, Harris PO, et al: Clinical use of the radioreceptor assay for neuroleptics. Psychiatry Res 2:173–178, 1980a

Cohen BM, Lipinski JF, Pope HG, et al: Neuroleptic blood levels and therapeutic effect. Psychopharmacology 70:191–193, 1980b

Cole JO, Goldberg SC, Davis JM: Drugs in the treatment of psychosis: controlled studies, in Psychiatric Drugs. Edited by Solomon P. New York, Grune & Stratton, 1966, pp 153–180

Conners CK, Barkley RA: Rating scales and checklists for child psychopharmacology. Psychopharmacol Bull 21:839–843, 1985

Creese I, Burt DR, Snyder SH: Dopamine receptor binding predicts clinical and pharmacological potencies of anti-schizophrenic drugs. Science 192:481–483, 1976

Davis JM, Schaffer CB, Killian GA, et al: Important issues in the drug treatment of schizophrenia. Schizophr Bull 6:70–87, 1980

Donlon PT, Hopkin JT, Tupin JP, et al: Haloperidol for acute schizophrenic inpatients. Arch Gen Psychiatry 37:691–695, 1980

Dysken MW, Javied JI, Chang SS, et al: Fluphenazine pharmacokinetics and therapeutic response. Psychopharmacology 73:205–210, 1981

Ericksen SE, Hurt SW, Chang S, et al: Haloperidol dose, plasma levels and clinical response: a double-blind study. Psychopharmacol Bull 14:15–16, 1978

Gardos G: Are antipsychotic drugs interchangeable? J Nerv Ment Dis 159:343–348, 1974

Garver DL, Dekirmenjian H, Davis JM, et al: Neuroleptic drug levels and therapeutic response: preliminary observations with red blood cell bound butaperazine. Am J Psychiatry 134:304–307, 1977

Garver DL, Hirschowitz J, Glicksteen GA, et al: Haloperidol plasma and red blood cell levels and clinical antipsychotic response. J Clin Psychopharmacol 4:133–137, 1984

Haase HJ: Extrapyramidal modification of fine movements: a "conditio sine qua non" of the fundamental therapeutic action of neuroleptic drugs, in Extrapyramidal System and Neuroleptics. Edited by Bordeleau JM. Montreal, Editions Psychiatriques, 1961, pp 329–353

Hyttel J, Larsen JJ, Christensen AV, et al: Receptor-binding profiles of neuroleptics, in Dyskinesia: Research and Treatment. Edited by Casey DE, Chase TN, Christensen AV, et al. Berlin, Springer-Verlag, 1985, pp 9–18

Itil TM, Keskiner A, Heinemann L, et al: Treatment of resistant schizophrenics with extreme high dosage fluphenazine hydrochloride. Psychosomatics 11:456–463, 1970

Kane JM: Treatment of schizophrenia. Schizophr Bull 13:133–156, 1987

Kane JM, Rifkin A, Quitkin F, et al: Antipsychotic drug blood levels and clinical response, in Progress in Psychiatric Drug Treatment, Vol 2. Edited by Klein D, Gittleman-Klein R. New York, Brunner/Mazel, 1976, pp 136–158

Magliozzi JR, Hollister LE, Arnold KV, et al: Relationship of serum haloperidol levels to clinical response in schizophrenic patients. Am J Psychiatry 138:365–367, 1981

Mavroidis ML, Kanter DR, Hirschowitz J, et al: Clinical response and plasma haloperidol levels in schizophrenia. Psychopharmacology 81:354–356, 1983

Mavroidis ML, Kanter DR, Hirschowitz J, et al: Therapeutic blood levels of fluphenazine: plasma or RBC determinations? Psychopharmacol Bull 20:168–170, 1984

May PRA, Van Putten T, Jenden DJ, et al: Chlorpromazine levels and the outcome of treatment in schizophrenic patients. Arch Gen Psychiatry 38:202–207, 1981

McCreadie RG, McDonald IM: High dosage haloperidol in chronic schizophrenia. Br J Psychiatry 131:310–316, 1977

McEvoy J, Stiller RL, Farr R: Plasma haloperidol levels drawn at neuroleptic threshold doses: a pilot study. J Clin Psychopharmacol 6:133–138, 1986

Morselli PL, Zarifian E, Cuche H, et al: Haloperidol plasma level monitoring in psychiatric patients, in Long-Term Effects of Neuroleptics: Advances in Biochemical Psychopharmacology, Vol 24. Edited by Cattabeni F, Racagni G, Spanop F, et al. New York, Raven, 1980, pp 529–536

Neborsky R, Janowsky D, Munson E, et al: Rapid treatment of acute psychotic symptoms with high- and low-dose haloperidol. Arch Gen Psychiatry 38:195–199, 1981

Neborsky RJ, Janowsky DS, Perel JM, et al: Plasma/RBC haloperidol ratios and improvement in acute psychotic symptoms. J Clin Psychiatry 45:10–13, 1984

Overall JE, Gorham DR: The Brief Psychiatric Rating Scale. Psychol Rep 10:799–812, 1962

Potkin SG, Shen Y, Zhou D, et al: Does a therapeutic window for plasma haloperidol exist: preliminary Chinese data. Psychopharmacol Bull 21:59–61, 1985

Quitkin F, Rifkin A, Klein D: Very high dosage versus standard dosage fluphenazine in schizophrenia: a double-blind study of non-chronic treatment-refractory patients. Arch Gen Psychiatry 32:1276–1281, 1975

Richelson E: Neuroleptic affinities for human brain receptors and their use in predicting adverse effects. J Clin Psychiatry 45:331–336, 1984

Rimon R, Averbuch I, Rozick P, et al: Serum and CSF levels of haloperidol by radioimmunoassay and radioreceptor assay during high-dose therapy of resistant schizophrenic patients. Psychopharmacology 73:197–199, 1981

Smith RC, Crayton J, Dekirmenjian H, et al: Blood levels of neuroleptic drugs in non-responding schizophrenic patients. Arch Gen Psychiatry 36:579–584, 1979

Smith RC, Baumgartner R, Ravichandran GK, et al: Plasma and cell levels of thioridazine and clinical response in schizophrenia. Psychiatry Res 12:287–296, 1984

Smith RC, Baumgartner R, Shvartsburd A, et al: Comparative efficacy of red cell and plasma haloperidol as predictors of clinical response in schizophrenia. Psychopharmacology 85:449–455, 1985

Van Putten T, Marder SR: Low-dose treatment strategies. J Clin Psychiatry 47(5S):12–16, 1986

Van Putten T, Marder SR, May PRA, et al: Plasma levels of haloperidol and clinical response. Psychopharmacol Bull 21:69–72, 1985

Wode-Helgodt B, Borg S, Fyro B, et al: Clinical effects and drug concentrations in plasma and cerebrospinal fluid in psychotic patients treated with fixed doses of chlorpromazine. Acta Psychiatr Scand 58:149–173, 1978

Chapter 5

Neuroleptic Plasma Levels in Treatment-Resistant Schizophrenic Patients

Theodore Van Putten, M.D.
Stephen R. Marder, M.D.
William Wirshing, M.D.
Kamal K. Midha, Ph.D., D.Sc.

Chapter 5

Neuroleptic Plasma Levels in Treatment-Resistant Schizophrenic Patients

In general clinical practice, the dosage of an antipsychotic drug used in the treatment of patients with schizophrenia is determined at best on a pragmatic "trial-and-error" basis. At worst, dosage is prescribed by rote. In many instances, dosage is adjusted upward until the patient either responds or develops toxic symptoms; in others, a fixed dosage is selected on the basis of "previous clinical experience." Much depends on "clinical impression." Some doctors prefer high doses and others prefer low doses; what dose-comparison studies there are (Cole 1982; Prien et al. 1972; Van Putten and May 1978) do not offer much of a guide in the usual patient.

These prescribing practices would be of little concern if the therapeutic index of the neuroleptics were wide—as is commonly assumed. More recent analyses of dose-response relationships (Baldessarini et al. 1988; Van Putten et al. 1987) indicate, however, that the therapeutic index of the neuroleptics is much narrower than formerly thought. If so, there is the possibility that some patients appear treatment resistant because they are on the wrong dosage.

It has been known for the past two decades that there is enormous (up to a 100-fold) variation in plasma levels of most neuroleptics in patients on the same dose (Dahl 1986; Midha et al. 1988). This raised the hope that plasma levels of neuroleptics could standardize dosing practices and that aberrant plasma levels could explain some cases of treatment resistance.

Much of the past research on the relation between plasma levels of antipsychotic drugs and clinical change, however, has been difficult to interpret because of shortcomings with the assays or because of design deficiencies—for example, lack of fixed-dose design, contamination with other treatments, or inclusion of treatment-resistant patients (Davis et al. 1978; May and Van Putten 1978). Regardless, one important question is whether the drug is bioavailable to the patient. Pi and Simpson (1981) even suggested that determinations of plasma level can provide laboratory evidence to extend and tighten the definition of refractory schizophrenia.

BIOAVAILABILITY AS A CAUSE OF TREATMENT FAILURE

Although *hypermetabolism, decreased absorption,* and *decreased bioavailability* are terms used by clinicians to justify high doses of neuroleptics, there are few examples in the literature that support decreased bioavailability as the cause of treatment failure.

Cooper et al. (1975) described a patient who responded well initially to butaperazine. During the ensuing weeks of therapy, however, the patient's clinical response to the same dose of butaperazine showed gradual deterioration, while steady-state levels of butaperazine fell until the drug was no longer detectable in his plasma. The authors suggested that decline in butaperazine level might be attributable to enzyme autoinduction and subsequent enhancement of metabolism. Smith et al. (1984) similarly noted two to seven times lower butaperazine plasma levels in chronic refractory inpatients than in patients who responded to butaperazine. Further, when the poor responders were given a test dose of butaperazine, peak plasma levels of butaperazine were again two to seven times lower than the peak butaperazine levels in the responding patients. Butaperazine, however, is no longer on the market.

Smith et al. (1979) also noted a strong correlation between steady-state levels of thioridazine and steady-state levels of butaperazine in the same nonresponding patients ($r = .74$, $P < .05$); patients with the lowest plasma butaperazine levels also had the lowest plasma thioridazine levels. Similarly, and in this same sample, 36 relative responders treated with oral haloperidol (15 mg/day) had mean ($\pm$ SE) steady-state plasma haloperidol levels of 15.3 ± 2.0 ng/ml after 1 week of treatment. This contrasts with the much lower haloperidol levels measured in six chronic nonresponders (mean, 4.0 ng/ml; range, 0–9 ng/ml) despite the fact that these nonresponders were treated with much higher doses of haloperidol (20–60 mg/day).

In a nonsystematic survey, Curry et al. (1970) reported very low chlorpromazine plasma levels in chronically hospitalized schizophrenic patients who had shown a consistently poor response to neuroleptic drugs. They reported on one patient taking chlorpromazine 600 mg/day who had a nondetectable plasma chlorpromazine level; this same patient showed very low chlorpromazine plasma levels following a 300-mg oral chlorpromazine test dose.

A dramatic illustration of enzyme induction was described by Hansen and Larsen (1982) in a letter to *The Lancet*. In this case, the patient was responding well to oral perphenazine until he started concomitant therapy with disulfiram. His clinical condition then deteriorated markedly, and his plasma level of perphenazine fell to about one-third of the steady-state level before disulfiram. At the same time, plasma concentrations of inactive sulfoxide metabolite were markedly elevated. Doubling the oral dose of perphenazine had little effect on either plasma concentrations or clinical condition. However, changing route of administration to intramuscular resulted in a substantial clinical improvement and an increase in plasma perphenazine concentrations to a therapeutic level. By contrast, perphenazine sulfoxide concentrations fell sharply. The authors suggested that disulfiram induced the enzyme(s) responsible for the sulfoxidation of perphenazine so much that most of the drug given by mouth was biotransformed to inactive metabolites. On the other hand, parenteral administration avoided the first-pass effect in the liver.

Carbamazepine is known to reduce plasma neuroleptic levels by 50% or more through microsomal enzyme induction (Ereshefsky et al. 1984; Jann et al. 1985). There is one reported case (Fast et al. 1986) of treatment failure secondary to this interaction.

Since most treatment-refractory patients, in public institutions at least, have been given a trial of treatment with fluphenazine decanoate (thereby avoiding the first-pass metabolism), it is very unlikely that decreased bioavailability is an adequate explanation for treatment failure except in an occasional patient. To confirm this, we examined the plasma levels in 12 long-stay treatment-refractory patients in a state hospital. These patients over the years were on high doses of haloperidol (40–420 mg/day) on the prescribing clinician's assumption that they were "hypermetabolizers" or "poor absorbers." In only two cases was the plasma haloperidol level low relative to dose (but not so low as to explain their treatment resistance), and the regression line of the high-dose patients was merely an extension of the regression line of newly admitted patients treated with more conventional doses of haloperidol (Van Putten et al. 1985). Since then, we have consulted on at least 30 more treatment-refractory patients on high doses (>30 mg/day), and in no case was the plasma level of haloperidol <15 ng/ml.

Although plasma levels of neuroleptics (at least in the case of haloperidol) in the treatment resistant are usually adequate, there remains the possibility that the drug is not available to the central nervous system because of excessive protein binding. It is well known that drugs such as chlorpromazine, trifluoperazine, thioridazine, and haloperidol are extensively bound to plasma proteins (Cohen et al. 1976; Forsman and Ohman 1977; Nyberg et al. 1978; Verbeeck et al. 1983). Consequently, only a small portion of the total drug in the plasma remains free from binding, although it is the "free fraction" that is responsible for therapeutic activity. Once again, there is interindividual variation in protein binding such that a 10-fold variation in plasma free fraction has been reported among individuals with identical total plasma concentrations of chlorpromazine (Curry 1970). The reason for this variation is that the acute-phase reactant alpha, acid glycoprotein (AGP) plays an important role in the binding of neuroleptic drugs (Piafsky 1980). The plasma concentration of AGP can show large fluctuations, even in the same individual, due to changes in normal physiologic functions and pathologic processes such as schizophrenia. Hence, the all-important free fraction of the drug in plasma will vary as the concentrations of the acute-phase reactant proteins change. Therefore, it may be important to take steps to establish the protein-binding status of refractory patients who appear to have adequate total levels of neuroleptic in their plasma. To date, this has not been investigated.

IDENTIFICATION OF BEHAVIORAL TOXICITY

Once it has been established that the drug is bioavailable to the refractory patient, the next question is whether the long-term use of neuroleptics may have led to the development of behavioral toxicity. If there is a "therapeutic window" relationship between neuroleptic plasma levels and clinical response, then some patients, at least in theory, could be refractory (or exhibit behavioral toxicity) because of excessively high plasma levels.

Behavioral toxicity secondary to neuroleptics is well documented. For example, the administration of phenothiazines can lead to the development of a catatonic-like stage (Gelenberg 1976; May 1959). Akathisia is often difficult to differentiate from psychotic excitement and can be associated with psychotic exacerbation (Van Putten and Marder 1987). Akinesia is very difficult (if not impossible) to differentiate from schizophrenic blunting, apathy, and withdrawal, and "akinetic depression" has been described (Van Putten and Marder 1987). Unsettled is whether behavioral toxicity is associated with unusually high plasma levels.

HIGH PLASMA LEVEL AND BEHAVIORAL TOXICITY

There have been a number of studies that describe therapeutic window relationships between neuroleptic plasma levels and clinical response (Dahl 1986). There are only a few reports, however, of patients with manifest psychotic symptoms concomitant with high plasma neuroleptic levels improving on dose reduction.

Rivera-Calimlim et al. (1973) reported that two patients who had plasma chlorpromazine concentrations of 750–1,000 ng/ml showed pronounced toxic symptoms (tremor, hypotension, and convulsions), and improved when the plasma concentrations were brought below 350 ng/ml. Van Putten et al. (1981) observed that four of six patients who became worse after a dose increase had chlorpromazine plasma concentrations well above 95 ng/ml. Three of these patients developed an agitated excitement and became assaultive. When the plasma chlorpromazine level was lowered, this behavior disappeared. Curry et al. (1970) also reported on a patient with a high (605 ng/ml) plasma level of chlorpromazine who remained "uncooperative, assaultive, fearful and hostile" (p. 293). Reduction of dosage by one-third (to 600 mg/day) resulted in a corresponding reduction in plasma level and in considerable and sustained improvement, characterized by reduction of fear and hostility and absence of assaultive behavior.

Extein et al. (1983) also reported a single patient in whom the initial antipsychotic effect of haloperidol was lost then regained as plasma levels went above (27.5 ng/ml) and then were brought back into the therapeutic window (10 ng/ml). Bjorndal et al. (1980) compared standard versus high dosage of haloperidol therapy in 22 male, relatively treatment-resistant chronic schizophrenic inpatients. Patients were randomly assigned to receive either 2-mg or 20-mg tablets of haloperidol. At the end of the trial, the dose of haloperidol in the standard-dosage group was 12–36 mg/day (mean, 15 mg/day); in the high-dosage group, the dose of haloperidol was 10–240 mg/day (mean, 103 mg/day). Three of the high-dosage patients with plasma levels above 100 ng/ml exhibited attacks of violent aggression during which they struck fellow patients and staff and damaged furniture. These attacks disappeared after a 50% reduction in plasma level. Further, depression (somatic concern, anxiety, guilt, and depressive mood) increased significantly during high-dosage treatment in the nonresponders. Schulz et al. (1984) reported a patient who improved on haloperidol 5 mg/day. On 5 mg of haloperidol, the patient had a surprisingly high plasma haloperidol level (22 ng/ml). When the dose of haloperidol was increased to 15 mg/day, the patient has a plasma level of 64 ng/ml and developed increased psychotic symptomatology. When plasma level was again lowered, the psychotic symptomatology improved.

The aforementioned cases indicate that, at least for some patients, there is behavioral toxicity at higher plasma levels. Further, these high plasma levels in some cases occurred at very ordinary dosages. Since treatment-refractory patients are usually on high doses of neuroleptic, it is likely that some would improve if dosage (and plasma level) were lowered. Clinically, one does encounter very treatment-resistant cases in whom a reduction of dosage is associated with marked improvement. The extent of this phenomenon is unknown; systematic research in which high plasma levels in treatment-resistant patients are systematically lowered is just getting started.

ASSAYS

High-performance liquid chromatography (HPLC) has been used increasingly and, since 1981, HPLC methods for nearly all neuroleptics have been available (Dahl 1986). Radioimmunoassays tend to be less precise but more sensitive than HPLC methods and are available for haloperidol (Rubin and Poland 1983) and fluphenazine (Midha et al. 1980). The radioreceptor assay is a new biological technique in which a neuroleptic drug and its dopamine-blocking metabolites compete with tritiated spiroperidol (or tritiated haloperidol) for dopamine D_2 binding sites on preparations of membranes from rat striatum. Theoretically, radioreceptor assay measures the total dopamine D_2 receptor blocking activity of drug and metabolites in the plasma or serum. Although theoretically attractive, the utility of the radioreceptor assay is unknown; it has only the promise of becoming useful to the practicing psychiatrist (Midha et al. 1987). At this time, the state of the art for measuring neuroleptic plasma levels is HPLC.

A NEW STUDY WITH HALOPERIDOL PLASMA LEVELS

The most work on the relation between plasma levels of neuroleptic and clinical response has been done with haloperidol. To detect a relationship between plasma levels of haloperidol (or any neuroleptic for that matter) and clinical response, patients need to be treated with a fixed dose(s) of haloperidol. Preferably, patients are randomly assigned to a low, an average, and a high dose so that both ends of the therapeutic window (if such exists) are represented. Variable dose studies tend to produce artifactual therapeutic windows (Van Putten and Marder 1986).

Four fixed-dose studies with haloperidol suggested a therapeutic window relationship between plasma haloperidol and clinical response; the suggested therapeutic ranges are 6.5–16 ng/ml (Smith et al. 1984), 3–11 ng/ml (Garver et al. 1984), 4–11 ng/ml (Mavroidis et al. 1983), and 4–22 ng/ml (Potkin et al. 1985). Seven fixed-dose studies did not find a therapeutic window relationship, but these studies were so designed that detection of a therapeutic window relationship (if such exists) was unlikely. Two studies (Bigelow et al. 1985; Rimon et al. 1981) used primarily poor neuroleptic responders. Four studies used such low doses—5 or 10 mg (Bleeker et al. 1984), 6 mg (Cohen and Baldessarini 1981; Itoh et al. 1984), and 0.2 mg/kg (Wistedt et al. 1984)—that detection of an upper toxic limit was unlikely. Two studies used doses too high—60 and 120 mg (Rimon et al. 1981) and 0.4 mg/kg (Bigelow et al. 1985)—to have plasma levels in the subtherapeutic range. The two studies (Cohen and Baldessarini 1981; Wistedt et al. 1984) with a low dose—6 mg (Cohen and Baldessarini 1981) and 0.2 mg/kg (Wistedt et al. 1984)—showed a linear relationship between clinical improvement and haloperidol levels, which may represent the ascending limb of the therapeutic window. In other words, of the 11 fixed-dose studies with haloperidol, 4, in retrospect, were designed properly, and these 4 found a therapeutic window.

In the four studies that suggested a therapeutic range (Garver et al. 1984; Mavroidis et al. 1983; Potkin et al. 1985; Smith et al. 1984), there are only a handful of cases that define the proposed toxic range. Further, these studies lack the clinically obvious: what is the clinical state of patients with toxic haloperidol levels? Do such patients appear overmedicated to start with? And, perhaps more compelling, do patients with toxic plasma levels improve when their plasma levels are lowered, and the converse?

The present study addresses these issues. The matter is important; if a therapeutic window relationship exists, it would have profound implications for clinical practice. In particular, the dose would be reduced in some nonresponding patients. More important, the usual dose of haloperidol for a psychotic inpatient is about 25 mg/day (Cohen and Baldessarini 1981), and, at this dose, a substantial portion of schizophrenic patients would be in the posited psychotoxic range (Van Putten et al. 1985).

Subjects and Methods

Subjects consisted of 67 newly (re)admitted drug-free (for at least 2 weeks, but usually several months) schizophrenic men (by DSM-III criteria [American Psychiatric Association 1980]) who were randomly assigned to receive haloperidol either 5, 10, or 20 mg/day for 4 weeks. In case of nonresponse, the doctor could increase (or decrease) the dose for another 4 weeks according to his or her clinical judgment. Clinical response was measured at baseline, weekly for the first 4 weeks, and at week 8 after the flexible-dose period. Clinical ratings were made blind to plasma levels.

On average, these patients were in their early 30s and had four previous hospitalizations. They had all served in the armed forces; had worked for an average of 4.5 years at some time in their life; were judged "markedly ill" on a nurses' rating scale; and scored at least "moderate" on conceptual disorganization, unusual thought content, or hallucinatory behavior. In fact, their mean baseline Brief Psychiatric Rating Scale (BPRS) (Overall and Gorham 1962) schizophrenia factor score was 13 (normal = 3; maximum = 21), indicating they were quite psychotic at baseline. The very excited or menacing patients were not included in this study; those who had a history of nonresponse to neuroleptics also were not included.

Figure 5-1 shows the actual scattergram of BPRS psychosis factor score versus haloperidol plasma level. It would appear that, on the average, clinical response decreases at plasma levels greater than 12 ng/ml. The "acid test," however, is whether patients with plasma levels greater than 12 ng/ml improve as their plasma levels are lowered.

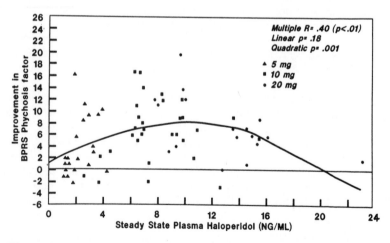

Figure 5-1. Curvilinear relation between steady-state plasma concentration of haloperidol and improvement (change from baseline) on the Brief Psychiatric Rating Scale psychotic factor score.

Reducing "Toxic" (>12 ng/ml) Plasma Level

At the end of the fixed-dose period, 13 patients had plasma levels greater than 12 ng/ml. Three insisted on leaving the hospital before a dosage adjustment was possible; all three had become more paranoid (mean ± SD BPRS paranoia factor score, − 3.5 ± 2.5), and two had become extremely dysphoric. One patient with a plasma level of 15.6 ng/ml insisted he required more haloperidol, and his plasma level eventually reached 90 ng/ml. The remaining nine patients, when their plasma level was reduced to less than 12 ng/ml, either experienced fewer side effects (in particular, a subjective sense of sedation and/or akinesia) or became less psychotic (five of eight), less dysphoric (three of eight), or less retarded (eight of eight). No patient deteriorated. Two patients had developed peculiar delusions of bodily destruction, which vanished as the plasma level was lowered. Table 5-1 summarizes the changes.

Raising the Plasma Level Above 12 ng/ml in Relative Nonresponders

In eight relative nonresponders with plasma levels in the 2–12 ng/ml range, the plasma level was raised above 12 ng/ml (range, 12.9–24 ng/ml; mean, 17.8 ng/ml). Six of eight cases became worse on the Clinical Global Impression (Guy 1976) ratings. On balance, these six became more dysphoric. Table 5-2 summarizes the changes.

The Lower Therapeutic Window Limit

Figure 5-1 suggests a lower limit of 2 ng/ml. If so, patients with plasma levels less than 2 ng/ml at the end of the fixed-dose period should improve as the plasma level is gradually raised. Patients with plasma levels of 1.8, 1.5, 1.6, 1.1, 1.1, and 1.4 ng/ml all improved (using the Clinical Global Impression as criterion) as their plasma levels rose above 2.0 ng/ml (the respective plasma levels at which

Table 5-1. Reducing "toxic" (>12 ng/ml) plasma levels: mean ± SD Brief Psychiatric Rating Scale factor change scores relative to baseline

Plasma level (ng/ml)	Schizophrenia[a]	Depression	Paranoia[b]	Retardation[c]
>12	5.1 ± 1.6	1.0 ± 4.3	2.4 ± 2.9	− 2.3 ± 3.4
<12	6.4 ± 2.2	2.8 ± 3.8	3.0 ± 3.5	− 0.1 ± 3.8

Note. Higher change scores mean more improvement.
[a]Two-tailed paired t = 2.76, P < .05. [b]Two-tailed paired t = 1.93, P < .10. [c]Two-tailed paired t = 5.34, P < .01.

"improvement" occurred were 2.9, 2.6, 2.1, 2.2, 2.0, and 6.7 ng/ml). One man with a plasma level of 1.8 ng/ml made a complete recovery. The two patients with plasma of 1.9 and 1.4 ng/ml did not improve at any plasma level, suggesting their illness was not sensitive to haloperidol.

Comment on Haloperidol Plasma Levels

A curvilinear relationship was found between plasma haloperidol and clinical response when patients were given fixed doses of haloperidol. The upper and lower limits of this proposed optimal range are, respectively, 12 and 2 ng/ml. When plasma levels in relative non-responders were pushed beyond 12 ng/ml (as in routine clinical practice), they, on balance, deteriorated. In particular, they became (relative to their status at the "therapeutic" plasma level) more dysphoric (BPRS depression factor, -2.6 ± 2.8, $P < .07$) and more withdrawn (BPRS withdrawal-retardation factor, -1.3 ± 2.6, not significant) and did not improve in global psychosis ratings (BPRS schizophrenia + paranoid factor, -0.83 ± 3.4, not significant).

Similarly, when patients with plasma levels greater than 12 ng/ml had their plasma levels lowered, they, on balance, improved (BPRS schizophrenia factor, $+1.25$, $P < .05$; BPRS withdrawal-retardation factor, $+2.1$, $P < .01$). No patient deteriorated. Some improved in the sense that they no longer appeared overmedicated in terms of a personal sense of sedation and/or objective akinesia. In these cases, a plasma level would only have confirmed what was already clinically apparent. Three patients with plasma levels greater than 12 ng/ml had become globally worse, developed a frantic agitation, and insisted on leaving the hospital before plasma levels could be lowered (two of these patients had become profoundly depressed). Finally, two patients had developed delusions of bodily destruction. One patient, at a plasma haloperidol level of 13.9 ng/ml, complained of "terminal syphilis" and a "weak heart." When the plasma haloperidol level was

Table 5-2. Pushing the plasma level in relative nonresponders: mean $\pm$ SD Brief Psychiatric Rating Scale factor change scores relative to baseline

Plasma level (ng/ml)	Schizophrenia	Depression[a]	Paranoia	Retardation
<12	1.67 ± 2.2	-1.2 ± 2.7	1.5 ± 2.3	0.3 ± 1.2
>12	2.7 ± 2.0	-3.8 ± 4.1	-0.3 ± 2.6	-1.0 ± 2.2

Note. Higher change scores mean more improvement; a negative ($-$) score means deterioration.
[a]Two-tailed paired $t = 2.33$, $P < .067$.

reduced to 8 ng/ml, these delusions disappeared. Another patient, at a plasma haloperidol level of 12.8 ng/ml, was suicidally preoccupied and complained that police officers had thrown "nerve gas" at him, thereby making him "all weak and shaky" and causing "ants to crawl on my bones." When the plasma haloperidol level was reduced to 6.3 ng/ml, these complaints disappeared. We believe, like Quitkin et al. (1975), that delusions of bodily destruction can be a psychotic rationalization of neuroleptic toxicity.

We do not mean to imply that patients with plasma levels above 12 ng/ml cannot improve relative to their baseline; after all, many schizophrenic patients in the United States are treated at plasma levels greater than 12 ng/ml. Table 5-3 dichotomizes patients into either "much" or "very much improved" versus "minimally improved," "no change," or "worse." Five patients were rated improved at plasma levels greater than 12 ng/ml. Also, some patients tolerated very high plasma levels. One 33-year-old man in this sample requested more and more haloperidol, claiming that each dosage increase made him feel somewhat better. Finally, at a dose of 90 mg of haloperidol (plasma level, 90 ng/ml), he became slightly sedated and developed moderate akathisia and dyskinesia, but remained much improved. When his plasma level was decreased to the therapeutic range, he remained improved and had fewer side effects (including a reduction in dyskinesia).

The proposed range of 2–12 ng/ml may not apply to the chronic, treatment-refractory patient. Certainly many such patients are stabilized at plasma levels of haloperidol much greater than 12 ng/ml (Van Putten et al. 1985). The fact that such patients, to varying degrees, can tolerate such high levels does not, however, mean that this is their optimal plasma level. Further, the higher plasma levels in some treatment-refractory patients are really utilized for "chemical restraint."

Table 5-3.   Global improvement at the end of the fixed-dose period

Plasma level (ng/ml)	Improved[a]	Not improved[b]
<2	1	10
2–12	26	17
>12	5	8

Note.   Likelihood ration $\chi^2 = 11.01$, $P = .004$.
[a]"Very much" or "much improved" on the Clinical Global Impression.
[b]"Minimal improvement," "no change," or "worse" on the Clinical Global Impression.

CONCLUSIONS

At this time, a neuroleptic plasma level is useful in demonstrating decreased bioavailability. A "nondetectable" or aberrantly low plasma level should result in the dose being increased or in switching to a depot-form of neuroleptic. Since most treatment-resistant patients, in public institutions at least, have had a trial of treatment with depot neuroleptics (which overcomes absorption problems and first-pass metabolism), it is unlikely that decreased bioavailability explains much treatment resistance. Decreased bioavailability is more likely to occur with concomitant administration of such known enzyme inducers as carbamazepine (which can lower neuroleptic levels by 50% or more), and other interactions are likely to be discovered.

Aberrantly high plasma levels in treatment-resistant patients are more problematic. In the case of haloperidol, a plasma level above 12 ng/ml should at least raise the possibility of reducing the dose. In the case of fluphenazine, two fixed-dose studies (Dysken et al. 1981; Mavroidis et al. 1984b) suggest that response may decrease above 2.0 ng/ml, but only a handful of patients had plasma levels above 2.0 ng/ml, and plasma fluphenazine level was not lowered into the therapeutic window to see if they would respond. In the case of chlorpromazine, plasma levels above 100 ng/ml may indeed be associated with behavioral toxicity (Van Putten et al. 1981).

In the case of thiothixene, a 2-week fixed-dose study of 19 patients taking thiothixene found a 40% or better improvement in 4 of 9 patients having plasma thiothixene levels in the range of 0.45–1.0 ng/ml, in 3 of 5 patients having levels in the range of 1.0–2.0 ng/ml,

Table 5-4.   Reported "therapeutic" plasma concentration ranges for antipsychotic drugs

Drug	Plasma concentration (ng/ml)
Chlorpromazine	30–100[a]
Fluphenazine	0.2–2.0[b]
Haloperidol	2–12[a]
Perphenazine	0.8–2.4[b]
Thiothixene	2.0–15[b]

[a]Consider dosage reduction in patients with plasma level above upper limit.
[b]Range of concentrations in which good response has been found; no evidence that reduction of plasma levels above the upper limit improves response.

and in all the 4 patients having levels in the range of 2.5–10 ng/ml. One patient with plasma levels of 22.2 and 15.3 ng/ml, after 1 and 2 weeks of treatment, respectively, became worse. It is unknown whether this patient would have improved at a lower plasma level (Mavroidis et al. 1984a). In the case of perphenazine, optimal antipsychotic effect with minimal extrapyramidal symptoms appears in the range of 0.8–2.4 ng/ml. Above this range, patients experience extrapyramidal symptoms with no gain (and possibly a loss) in antipsychotic effect (Bolvig Hansen and Larsen 1983; 1985; Bolvig Hansen et al. 1982). In the case of thioridazine, the only fixed-dose study as of this writing found no relationship between plasma concentration and therapeutic response (Smith et al. 1985).

Table 5-4 summarizes reported therapeutic plasma concentrations for some antipsychotic drugs. These therapeutic plasma levels concentrations cannot be regarded as established by any means, but may help to identify aberrant plasma levels.

The facts are that the utility of high neuroleptic plasma levels in the treatment-resistant patient has not been investigated. Studies that seek to establish a relationship between plasma level and clinical response must exclude treatment-resistant patients, because no relationship between clinical response and plasma level can be demonstrated if a substantial portion of the sample is truly treatment resistant. Further, the relationship between plasma level and clinical state in the chronic treatment-refractory patient is likely to be complicated. The setting and psychological requirements of the individual patient may affect plasma level requirements. Thus, in some treatment-resistant patients, particularly in poorly staffed institutions, high plasma levels are really utilized for "chemical restraint," conceptualized as a combination of akinesia and sedation. Chemical restraint can also be the least restrictive form of treatment for a patient who is aggressive in response to intractable hallucinations or delusions. Also, some treatment-resistant patients actually prefer sedation and akinesia to dampen their misery or to help contain destructive impulses. Studies in which treatment-refractory patients with high plasma levels are randomly assigned to plasma level reduction or to a control group in which plasma level remains the same are much needed.

REFERENCES

American Psychiatric Association: Diagnostic and Statistical Manual of Mental Disorders, 3rd Edition. Washington, DC, American Psychiatric Association, 1980

Baldessarini RJ, Cohen BM, Teicher MH: Significance of neuroleptic dose and plasma level in the pharmacological treatment of psychoses. Arch Gen Psychiatry 45:79–91, 1988

Bigelow LB, Kirch DG, Braun T, et al: Absence of relationship of serum haloperidol concentration and clinical response in chronic schizophrenia: a fixed-dose study. Psychopharmacol Bull 21:66–68, 1985

Bjorndal N, Bjerre M, Gerlach J, et al: High dosage haloperidol therapy in chronic schizophrenic patients: a double-blind study of clinical response, side effects, serum haloperidol, and serum prolactin. Psychopharmacology 67:17–23, 1980

Bleeker JAC, Dingemans PM, Frohn-De Winder ML: Plasma level and effect of low-dose haloperidol in acute psychosis. Psychopharmacol Bull 20:317–319, 1984

Bolvig Hansen L, Larsen N-E: Plasma levels of perphenazine related to clinical effect and extrapyramidal side-effects, in Clinical Pharmacology in Psychiatry: Bridging the Experimental-Therapeutic Gap. Edited by Gram, Usdin E, Dahl SG. London, Macmillan, 1983, pp 175–181

Bolvig Hansen L, Larsen N-E: Therapeutic advantages of monitoring plasma concentrations of perphenazine in clinical practice. Psychopharmacology 87:16–19, 1985

Bolvig Hansen L, Larsen N-E, Gulman N: Dose-response relationships of perphenazine in the treatment of acute psychoses. Psychopharmacology 78:112–115, 1982

Cohen BM, Baldessarini RJ: Haloperidol and clinical response. Am J Psychiatry 138:1513–1514, 1981

Cohen BM, Herschel M, Aoba A: Neuroleptic, antimuscarinic and antiadrenergic activity of chlorpromazine, thioridazine and their metabolites. Psychiatry Res 1:199–208, 1976

Cole JO: Antipsychotic drugs: is more better? McLean Hospital 7:6–7, 1982

Cooper TB, Simpson GM, Haher EJ, et al: Butaperazine pharmacokinetics. Arch Gen Psychiatry 32:903–905, 1975

Curry SH: Plasma protein binding of chlorpromazine. Journal of Pharmacy and Pharmacology 22:193–197, 1970

Curry SH, Marshall JHL, Davis JM, et al: Chlorpromazine plasma levels and effects. Arch Gen Psychiatry 22:289–296, 1970

Dahl SG: Plasma level monitoring of antipsychotic drugs: clinical utility. Clin Pharmacokinet 11:36–61, 1986

Davis JM, Erikson S, Dekirmenjian H: Plasma levels of antipsychotic drugs and clinical response, in Psychopharmacology: A Generation of Progress. Edited by Lipton MA, DiMascio A, Killam KF. New York, Raven, 1978, pp 905–915

Dysken MW, Javaid JI, Chang SS, et al: Fluphenazine pharmacokinetics and therapeutic response. Psychopharmacology 73:205–210, 1981

Ereshefsky L, Davis CM, Harrington CA: Haloperidol and reduced haloperidol plasma levels in selected schizophrenic patients. J Clin Psychopharmacol 4:138–142, 1984

Extein I, Pottash ALC, Gold MS: Therapeutic window for plasma haloperidol in acutely schizophrenic psychosis. Lancet 1:1048–1049, 1983

Fast DK, Jones BD, Kusalic M, et al: Effect of carbamazepine on neuroleptic plasma level and efficacy (letter). Am J Psychiatry 143:117–118, 1986

Forsman A, Ohman R: Studies on serum protein binding of haloperidol. Current Therapeutic Research 21:245–255, 1977

Garver DL, Hirschowitz J, Glicksteen GA, et al: Haloperidol plasma and red blood cell levels and clinical antipsychotic response. J Clin Psychopharmacol 4:133–137, 1984

Gelenberg AJ: The catatonic syndrome. Lancet 1:1339–1341, 1976

Guy W: ECDEU Assessment Manual for Psychopharmacology. Rockville, MD, National Institute of Mental Health Psychopharmacology Research Branch, 1976

Hansen LB, Larsen NE: Metabolic interaction between perphenazine and disulfiram (letter). Lancet 2:1472, 1982

Itoh H, Yagi G, Fujii Y, et al: The relationship between haloperidol blood levels and clinical responses. Prog Neuropsychopharmacol Biol Psychiatry 8:285–292, 1984

Jann MW, Ereshefsky L, Saklad SR: Effects of carbamazepine on plasma haloperidol levels. J Clin Psychopharmacol 5:106–109, 1985

Mavroidis ML, Kanter DR, Hirschowitz J, et al: Clinical response and plasma haloperidol levels in schizophrenia. Psychopharmacology 81:354–356, 1983

Mavroidis ML, Kanter DR, Hirschowitz J, et al: Clinical relevance of thiothixene plasma levels. J Clin Psychopharmacol 4:155–157, 1984a

Mavroidis ML, Kanter DR, Hirschowitz J, et al: Fluphenazine plasma levels and clinical response. J Clin Psychiatry 45:370–373, 1984b

May RH: Catatonic-like states following phenothiazine therapy. Am J Psychiatry 115:1119–1120, 1959

May PRA, Van Putten T: Plasma and saliva levels of chlorpromazine in schizophrenia: a critical view of the literature. Arch Gen Psychiatry 35:1081–1087, 1978

Midha KK, Cooper JK, Hubbard JW: Radioimmunoassay for fluphenazine in human plasma. Communications in Psychopharmacology 4:107–114, 1980

Midha KK, Hawes EM, Hubbard JW, et al: The search for correlations between neuroleptic plasma levels and clinical outcome: a critical review, in Psychopharmacology: The Third Generation of Progress. Edited by Meltzer HY. New York, Raven, 1987

Midha KK, Hubbard JW, May PRA: The role of the analytical biochemist in resistant schizophrenia, in Treatment Resistance in Schizophrenia. Edited by Dencker SJ, Kulhanek F. Braunschweig/Wiesbaden, Vieweg, 1988

Nyberg G, Axelson R, Martenson E: Binding of thioridazine and thioridazine metabolites to serum proteins in psychiatric patients. Eur J Clin Pharmacol 14:341–350, 1978

Overall JE, Gorham DR: The Brief Psychiatric Rating Scale. Psychol Rep 10:799–812, 1962

Pi EH, Simpson GM: The treatment of refractory schizophrenia: pharmacotherapy and clinical implications of blood level measurement of neuroleptics. International Pharmacopsychiatry 16:154–161, 1981

Piafsky KF: Disease induced changes in the plasma binding of basic drugs. Clin Pharmacokinet 5:246–262, 1980

Potkin SG, Shen Y, Zhou D, et al: Does a therapeutic window for plasma haloperidol exist: preliminary Chinese data. Psychopharmacol Bull 21:59–61, 1985

Prien RF, Levin J, Cole JO: Indication for high dose chlorpromazine therapy in chronic schizophrenia, in Annual Review of the Schizophrenic Syndrome. Edited by Cancro R. New York, Brunner/Mazel, 1972

Quitkin F, Rifkin A, Klein DF: Very high dosage vs standard dosage fluphenazine in schizophrenia. Arch Gen Psychiatry 32:1276–1281, 1975

Rimon R, Averbuch I, Rozick P, et al: Serum and CSF levels of haloperidol by radioimmunoassay and radioreceptor assay during high-dose therapy of resistant schizophrenic patients. Psychopharmacology 73:197–199, 1981

Rivera-Calimlim R, Casteneda L, Lasagna L: Effects of mode of management on plasma chlorpromazine in psychiatric patients. Clin Pharmacol Ther 14:978–986, 1973

Rubin R, Poland RE: Serum haloperidol determinations and their contribution to the treatment of schizophrenia, in Clinical Pharmacology: Bridging the Experimental-Therapeutic Gap. Edited by Gram et al. London, Macmillan, 1983, pp 217–225

Schulz SC, Butterfield L, Garicano M, et al: Beyond the therapeutic window: a case presentation. J Clin Psychiatry 45:223–225, 1984

Smith RC, Crayton J, Dekirmenjian H, et al: Blood levels of neuroleptic drugs in nonresponding chronic schizophrenic patients. Arch Gen Psychiatry 36:579–584, 1979

Smith RC, Baumgartner R, Misra CH, et al: Haloperidol, plasma levels and prolactin response as predictors of clinical improvement in schizophrenia: chemical vs radioreceptor plasma level assay. Arch Gen Psychiatry 41:1044–1049, 1984

Smith RC, Baumgartner R, Burd A, et al: Haloperidol and thioridazine drug levels and clinical response in schizophrenia: comparison of gas-liquid chromatography and radioreceptor drug level assays. Psychopharmacol Bull 21:52–58, 1985

Van Putten T, Marder SR: Variable dose studies provide misleading therapeutic windows. J Clin Psychopharmacol 6:249–250, 1986

Van Putten T, Marder SR: Behavioral toxicity of EPS. J Clin Psychiatry (Suppl) 48:13–19, 1987

Van Putten T, May PRA: Akinetic depression in schizophrenia. Arch Gen Psychiatry 35:1101–1107, 1978

Van Putten T, May PRA, Jenden DJ: Does a plasma level of chlorpromazine help? Psychol Med 11:729–734, 1981

Van Putten T, Marder SR, May PRA, et al: Plasma levels of haloperidol and clinical response. Psychopharmacol Bull 21:59–72, 1985

Van Putten T, Marder SR, Mintz J: The therapeutic index of haloperidol in newly admitted schizophrenic patients. Psychopharmacol Bull 23:201–207, 1987

Verbeeck RK, Cardinal JA, Hill AG, et al: Binding of phenotiazine neuroleptics to plasma proteins. Biochem Pharmacol 32:2565–2570, 1983

Wistedt B, Johanidesz G, Omerhodzic M, et al: Plasma haloperidol levels and clinical response in acute schizophrenia. Nordisk Psychiatr Tidsskr 1:9–13, 1984

Chapter 6

Benzodiazepine Augmentation of Neuroleptics

Owen M. Wolkowitz, M.D.
Mark H. Rapaport, M.D.
David Pickar, M.D.

Chapter 6

Benzodiazepine Augmentation of Neuroleptics

Torrey (1980) called schizophrenia "the cruelest disease of the Western world. It afflicts young adults, often beginning insidiously and progressing until the ambitions, potentials, and hopes of early years are discarded in disarray. In their place lie broken thoughts, inappropriate or stunted emotions, and internal voices or other misperceptions that can make existence a living hell" (p. 3). Fortunately, medical science has been able to intervene pharmacologically in the treatment of these patients to decrease their symptomatology and improve their functioning (Davis 1980). Since their introduction in the mid-1950s, neuroleptics have been the mainstay of the pharmacologic treatment of schizophrenia; however, several problems exist that limit their usefulness. Neuroleptics are associated with troublesome and occasionally disabling acute and chronic side effects such as dystonias, tardive dyskinesia, akathisia, autonomic side effects, and neuroleptic malignant syndrome (Davis 1980; Pickar 1986). Further, in the majority of patients, specific schizophrenic symptoms are only partially responsive to neuroleptic treatment. For example, "positive" and "negative" symptoms may respond differentially in given patients (Breier et al. 1987b; Pickar et al. 1987); therefore neuroleptic treatment is best considered palliative rather than curative in most patients. Inadequate symptom resolution may be particularly worrisome since a major determinant of outcome in schizophrenic patients is the amount of positive and negative symptomatology that is resistant to neuroleptic treatment (Breier et al. 1987a). Finally, approximately 10–30% of patients with schizophrenia show poor or no response to neuroleptic medication (Davis 1980); in the United States alone, there are approximately one-half million such neuroleptic nonresponders.

Supported in part by NIHM First Independent Research Support and Transition award MH-43612 to Dr. Wolkowitz.

In an attempt to address these concerns, pharmacologic strategies aimed at enhancing neuroleptic response have been developed. Although clinicians typically eschew the use of multidrug regimens, a number of agents added to neuroleptics, such as lithium, carbamazepine, benzodiazepines, reserpine, and others have been shown to improve or "augment" neuroleptic response in some patients (Pickar 1986). Given the presumed heterogeneity of schizophrenia and the importance of symptom reduction, any treatment that consistently benefits even a small proportion of patients is worth pursuing.

Controlled trials of benzodiazepines in the treatment of schizophrenia began nearly 25 years ago and were prompted by their well-recognized tranquilizing effects. Since that time, a large body of evidence has accumulated regarding their efficacy as adjunctive treatments in schizophrenia (Arana et al. 1986; Donaldson et al. 1983; Nestoros 1980). As with most of the augmenting agents, benzodiazepines are generally more effective when co-administered with neuroleptics than when administered alone and are helpful only to a proportion of patients treated. The fact that individual patients respond differently to different augmenting agents implies differences in biological substrates. As we will discuss, study of these differences affords an opportunity to characterize the biological heterogeneity of schizophrenia.

The purpose of this chapter is to review and synthesize the findings of the clinical studies with benzodiazepines. We have, out of necessity, been selective in our review; we have focused on double-blind, placebo-controlled studies and have subgrouped them according to type of benzodiazepine used (low potency versus high potency versus triazolobenzodiazepines). We have also chosen to present more detailed discussion of our own studies to underscore certain themes or highlight certain findings. We first explore the theoretical rationales for using benzodiazepines in the treatment of schizophrenia. We next examine clinical studies in which behavioral responses to benzodiazepine augmentation were assessed. In the third part of the chapter, we focus on predictor variables and biological "markers" of clinical response. We concluded the chapter with a discussion of the clinical implications of the reviewed literature and with questions that remain to be answered.

THEORETICAL RATIONALES

In using benzodiazepines in schizophrenia, two perspectives are conceptualized in explaining their efficacy. By reducing anxiety, benzodiazepines help patients with prominent anxiety symptoms; in acutely agitated patients, benzodiazepines have sedating effects (Salzman 1988). Indeed, retrospective and prospective studies have found benzodiazepines to be efficacious in this context and to allow the administration of lower doses of neuroleptics (Salzman et al. 1986). In addition to having antianxiety and sedating effects, benzodiazepines may have more specific antipsychotic effects via two additional mechanisms. Animal studies have shown that benzodiazepines decrease presynaptic dopamine release in the brain (Singhal et al. 1983; Wood 1982) and also modulate the stress/benzodiazepine-sensitive prefrontal cortical dopamine system (Deutch et al. 1985; Lavielle et al. 1978; Tam and Roth 1985).

The dopamine hypothesis of schizophrenia is based largely on two bodies of evidence. Clinically effective neuroleptics induce an increase in the accumulation of dopamine metabolites in the rat brain (Carlsson and Lindquist 1963), suggesting a compensatory increase in dopamine release in response to transmission blockade. Further, clinically effective neuroleptics have been demonstrated to bind to postsynaptic dopamine (D_2) receptors, and their ability to competitively displace tritiated haloperidol binding to these receptors correlates with their clinical potency (Creese et al. 1976). One problem with the dopamine hypothesis is that, whereas dopamine postsynaptic receptor blockade occurs very rapidly after administration of neuroleptics, maximum clinical effects of neuroleptics are not observed for several weeks. A more recent elaboration of the dopamine hypothesis proposes that neuroleptic-induced postsynaptic receptor blockade is the first action in a chain of events that ultimately leads to a decrease in presynaptic dopamine release; the time course of this decrease in dopamine release more closely parallels that of clinical efficacy (Pickar 1988; Pickar et al. 1984, 1986). Animal and human studies indicate that neuroleptics acutely increase dopamine turnover, reflected by increased levels of homovanillic acid (HVA). Over time, dopaminergic systems become tolerant to this effect, and HVA levels fall back to or below baseline levels, perhaps as a result of "depolarization blockade" (Roth 1983). Benzodiazepines have been found to blunt the acute neuroleptic-induced rise in HVA in the rat brain (Keller et al. 1976), and thus might be expected to facilitate or expedite those clinical responses dependent on decreases in presynaptic dopamine release. Benzodiazepines also shift to the left the dose-response curve relating haloperidol doses to catalepsy in rats, providing behavioral evidence that benzodiazepines, added to neuroleptics, further decrease dopamine activity at the postsynaptic receptor (Keller et al. 1976).

Aside from this quantitative explanation of how benzodiazepines might augment neuroleptics, there is a more qualitative one. Four major dopaminergic tracts have been identified in the brain: the tuberoinfundibular, the nigrostriatal, the mesolimbic, and the mesocortical. There are several unique properties of the mesocortical dopamine tract. Of particular note, these neurons lack autoreceptors and have diminished responsiveness to neuroleptics, as evidenced by a diminished increase in dopamine synthesis and accumulation acutely and a resistance to the development of biochemical tolerance chronically (Bannon and Roth 1983). This is in marked contrast to the pattern of acute increases followed by chronic decreases in dopamine activity, described above, which are seen in the nigrostriatal and mesolimbic pathways. In addition, the mesocortical dopamine neurons have a heightened sensitivity to stress and to benzodiazepines in animals, evidenced by a preferential activation by mild foot shock stress and by benzodiazepine receptor inverse agonists, the beta-carbolines. Further, benzodiazepines inhibit this stress activation; these benzodiazepine effects are blocked by Ro 15-1788, a benzodiazepine receptor antagonist, implicating benzodiazepine receptors in these effects (Lavielle et al. 1978; Tam and Roth 1985). Petty et al. (1987) demonstrated that alprazolam, a triazolobenzodiazepine, significantly reduced haloperidol-induced increases in dopamine metabolism in the frontal cortex, but not the caudate, of living rats. Benzodiazepines, therefore, may be particularly effective in decreasing dopamine activity in precisely that dopamine tract where neuroleptics are the least effective.

EMPIRICAL STUDIES: REVIEW OF LITERATURE

Twelve double-blind studies have evaluated the efficacy of benzodiazepines as adjunctive treatments in combination with neuroleptics in the treatment of schizophrenia. Of these studies, six reported some positive effects (Altamura et al. 1987; Guz et al. 1972; Kellner et al. 1975; Lingjaerde 1982; Lingjaerde et al. 1979; Wolkowitz et al. 1988), three reported negative effects (Hanlon et al. 1969, 1970; Karson et al. 1982), and three reported mixed effects (Csernansky et al. 1988; Holden et al. 1968; Michaux et al. 1966). It must be noted that many of the early studies had methodological flaws, including nonuniform diagnoses, nonspecific rating scales, and poor statistical analyses. When only those studies conducted since 1975 are examined, six of the seven studies (Altamura et al. 1987; Csernansky et al. 1988; Kellner et al. 1975; Lingjaerde 1982; Lingjaerde et al. 1979; Wolkowitz et al. 1988) reported some positive effects, although in some of the studies the positive effects were modest, transient, or specific for certain symptoms. These studies examined the effects of different benzodiazepines, and it is unknown if specific benzodiazepines are more clinically effective than others. For this reason, we have grouped the studies by the type of benzodiazepine used in the following discussion.

Low-Potency Benzodiazepines

Csernansky et al. (1988) studied 55 schizophrenic outpatients selected on the basis of having at least mild negative symptoms. Patients received diazepam (average dose, 39 mg/day) or placebo, added to stable doses of neuroleptics for up to 6 weeks. At both 2 and 6 weeks, diazepam treatment was not significantly different from placebo on ratings of either positive or negative schizophrenic symptoms. Lingjaerde et al. (1979) studied 23 patients with chronic schizophrenia or reactive psychoses whose symptoms were only partially responsive to neuroleptics alone. Diazepam (15 mg/day) or placebo was added to previously stabilized neuroleptic regimens in a crossover design. Diazepam was significantly better than placebo in reducing Brief Psychiatric Rating Scale (Overall and Gorham 1961) total ratings and the individual items of suspiciousness and unusual thought content. Kellner et al. (1975) studied six patients with schizophrenia with prominent anxiety symptoms that were not relieved by increasing doses of neuroleptics. Only patients who first responded to open-label chlordiazepoxide (300 mg/day) and who relapsed on placebo were included in the study. In their study, chlordiazepoxide (150–300 mg/day) or placebo was added to stable neuroleptic regimens in a multiple crossover (intensive) design. Three of the six patients showed significant improvement with chlordiazepoxide; in two of these, the improvement was "striking." Hallucinations, suspiciousness, and unusual thought content improved in addition to anxiety. Two patients showed no change, and one showed a nonsignificant increase in depression. They found that initial anxiety levels were directly correlated with clinical improvement.

High-Potency Benzodiazepines

Altamura et al. (1987) added clonazepam (3 mg/day) or placebo to the haloperidol regimens of 24 patients with schizophrenia. Clonazepam resulted in an earlier improvement in total Brief Psychiatric Rating Scale scores than did placebo. This earlier improvement was due largely to improvements in anxiety, tension, and excitement, and not to improvements in psychotic symptoms per se. No significant difference was observed between clonazepam and placebo after 4 weeks of treatment. Additionally, clonazepam was associated with significantly fewer extrapyramidal symptoms and akathisia throughout the study. In the one study in which clear negative effects were observed, Karson et al. (1982) observed that four of nine chronic schizophrenic patients treated with adjunctive clonazepam (various doses) versus placebo worsened (became more aggressive). No significant effects were observed on thought disorder, withdrawal, paranoia, anxiety, depression, or activity.

Triazolobenzodiazepines

Lingjaerde (1982) studied 51 patients with auditory hallucinations who were resistant to treatment with neuroleptics (46 with schizophrenia, 2 with manic depression, 3 with reactive psychosis). The patients were administered estazolam (6 mg/day), a triazolobenzodiazepine, or placebo added to neuroleptics in a crossover design. Estazolam was found to be significantly superior to placebo on the specific items of auditory hallucination frequency, visual hallucinations, and compulsive thoughts. In the study by Csernansky et al. (1988) described above, in which patients were treated with diazepam or placebo, an additional group of patients was treated with alprazolam (average dose, 3.7 mg/day). During the first weeks of the study, alprazolam was significantly superior to placebo and to diazepam in decreasing withdrawal-retardation (negative symptom) ratings on the Brief Psychiatric Rating Scale. By the end of the study, however, alprazolam was not significantly different from placebo or diazepam on this measure, and at no point did it produce significant improvements in ratings of positive symptoms. The authors noted, however, that individual alprazolam-treated patients showed enduring benefits throughout the study.

We also reported the results of a study of alprazolam augmentation of fluphenazine in a group of 12 treatment-resistant schizophrenic inpatients (Wolkowitz et al. 1986, 1988). In this study alprazolam was added in a double-blind manner to stable doses of fluphenazine hydrochloride and increased up to individually determined optimum doses (mean, 2.87 mg/day; range, 1.5–5.0 mg/day). Ratings of psychotic and other symptoms—Brief Psychiatric Rating Scale; Bunney-Hamburg Global Ratings of psychosis, anxiety, and depression (Bunney and Hamburg 1963); and Abrams and Taylor Rating Scale of emotional blunting (Abrams and Taylor 1978), a measure of "negative" symptoms—were performed at baseline (fluphenazine plus placebo), during the first 2 weeks of alprazolam augmentation, during the optimum-dose alprazolam period, during the final 2 weeks of alprazolam withdrawal (0.5 mg decrease every 3 days), and finally during the post-alprazolam fluphenazine plus placebo treatment period. Fluphenazine and antiparkinsonian doses were held constant throughout the study. As can be seen in Figure 6-1, significant reductions were observed in Bunney-Hamburg global psychosis and Brief Psychiatric Rating Scale positive symptom subscale ratings during the optimum-dose alprazolam-treatment period compared to both baseline periods. Clinical improvement did not seem related to sedation or psychomotor retardation. Although some individual patients experienced "rebound" worsening of psychotic symptoms following alprazolam withdrawal, there was no significant group mean effect in this direction. Although no significant group mean effects were observed on Bunney-Hamburg global ratings of anxiety or depression or on Abrams and Taylor Rating Scale ratings of negative symptoms in the optimum-dose period compared to the initial-baseline period, the changes in all of these ratings were significantly correlated with the changes in Bunney-Hamburg global psychosis ratings, suggesting that responsive patients also showed improvements in anxiety, depression, and negative symptoms.

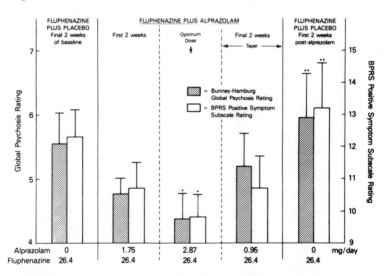

Figure 6-1. Changes in mean ± SE Bunney-Hamburg global psychosis ratings (*shaded bars*) and Brief Psychiatric Rating Scale (BPRS) positive symptom subscale ratings (*open bars*) associated with alprazolam treatment and withdrawal. Mean alprazolam and fluphenazine hydrochloride doses are at bottom. Analyses of variance: global psychosis ratings ($F = 3.89$, 4/44 df, $P < .01$) BPRS positive symptom subscale ratings: ($F = 3.77$, 4/44 df, $P < .01$). *$P < .05$ compared with baseline (post hoc t test); † $P < .05$ compared with optimum-dose alprazolam treatment (post hoc t test) (Wolkowitz et al. 1988).

Our finding of a significant group mean effect on clinical ratings should not obscure the fact that we found distinct responders and nonresponders among individual patients. Of the 12 patients, 7 exhibited some benefit with alprazolam augmentation (reductions of 20–47% in Bunney-Hamburg global psychosis ratings); 5 of these demonstrated clinically significant benefit and were termed *responders*. Five patients exhibited no benefit (increases of 0–25% in Bunney-Hamburg global psychosis ratings) and were termed *nonresponders*.

More recently, we presented preliminary data from a larger-scale double-blind replication study being conducted at the University of California, San Francisco (Wolkowitz et al. 1989). To date, we have added alprazolam (mean dose, 3 mg/day) or placebo to stabilized neuroleptic regimens in nine treatment-resistant schizophrenic inpatients and have continued to observe a significant advantage of alprazolam in reducing psychotic symptoms. Two of our best alprazolam responders were discharged from the hospital on alprazolam and, at 6- and 9-month open-label follow-up, have continued to do better than prior to entering the study. There has been no evidence of dosage tolerance in either patient.

SUMMARY OF LITERATURE REVIEW

Several of these double-blind studies have suggested therapeutic effects of benzodiazepines added to neuroleptics in the treatment of schizophrenia. However, the effects may be seen in only certain patients and may be modest, transient, and selective for particular symptoms. We next discuss several issues that bear on our interpretation of the studies we have reviewed.

Do Benzodiazepines Differ in Efficacy?

There does not seem to be clear evidence from these double-blind studies that high-potency benzodiazepines are superior to low-potency benzodiazepines in the treatment of schizophrenia. Indeed, the two studies reviewed here suggest that the high-potency benzodiazepine, clonazepam, is either ineffective (or detrimental) or may result in transient improvements in anxiety symptoms and in improvements in extrapyramidal symptoms and akathisia rather than in psychotic symptoms per se. There is a suggestion, which must remain tentative at this time, that triazolobenzodiazepines are slightly superior to other benzodiazepines in augmenting neuroleptics. This is supported by the only study as of this writing that has directly compared alprazolam to diazepam (Csernansky et al. 1988), and by the personal observations of Lingjaerde (1985). There may indeed be some reason to suspect different responses to triazolobenzodiazepines compared to other benzodiazepines. These agents, while having comparable antianxiety, anticonvulsant, and muscle relaxant effects, additionally have antidepressant and antipanic effects and have some unique biochemical and electrophysiologic properties (Dawson et al. 1984).

Specificity of Response

Several of the studies reviewed here noted benzodiazepine-associated improvements in anxiety, tension, and excitement, and one noted transient improvement in negative symptoms. Others, however, noted improvement in core psychotic symptoms such as hallucinations, delusions, and thought disorder. In our own study, we observed the most significant improvements in positive psychotic symptoms with only partial evidence of improvements in anxiety, depression, and negative symptoms. Possible sources of variability in clinical response to benzodiazepines are discussed below, but it does appear that individual patients may demonstrate clinically significant antipsychotic responses to benzodiazepine augmentation. One of the studies reviewed also noted benzodiazepine-associated improvements in extrapyramidal symptoms and akathisia. Since these side effects may mimic psychotic symptoms, future studies must carefully dissect benzodiazepine effects on extrapyramidal symptoms and akathisia from those on actual psychotic symptoms. It should also be noted that several studies with alprazolam augmentation (Csernansky et al. 1984; Douyon et al. 1989; Kahn et al. 1988; Wolkowitz et al. 1986); have commented on clinical changes in individual patients that are not characteristic of neuroleptic effects, such as improvements in social and emotional relatedness, spontaneity, sociability, affability, humor, and increased interest in family and social life. In our experience, when such changes occur, they develop rapidly (within the first 2 weeks) and may be striking.

Longevity of Response

There have been no controlled studies as of this writing of extended or maintenance treatment of schizophrenic patients with benzodiazepines added to neuroleptics. Two of the studies presented here found the beneficial effects to be short-lived (less than 2 weeks); others noted more long-lasting effects. Anecdotal evidence (Csernansky et al. 1988; Wolkowitz et al. 1989); suggests that individual patients may show more long-lasting benefits, but this remains to be tested in future studies.

Dose Response and Pharmacokinetic Considerations

Few studies have examined dose-response relationships in benzodiazepine treatment of schizophrenia or possible benzodiazepine-neuroleptic pharmacokinetic interactions. Csernansky et al. (1988) reported that mean plasma alprazolam levels were inversely correlated with withdrawal-retardation ratings, although those results were largely determined by two outlying patients. In an open-label trial of alprazolam augmentation in treatment-resistant schizophrenics, Douyon et al. (1989) similarly found that patients with higher plasma alprazolam levels (greater than 23 ng/ml) responded more favorably (with reductions in ratings of positive and negative symptoms) than did patients with lower levels, and they raised the possibility of adjusting alprazolam doses to achieve plasma levels of 60–80 ng/ml. They also observed that alprazolam increased haloperidol or fluphenazine levels by an average of 23%, but they suggested that the clinical effects they observed were not secondary to this. In our study (Wolkowitz et al. 1988), we found that clinical response was not correlated with plasma alprazolam levels; the average plasma alprazolam level attained in our responders was only 18.5 ng/ml. We also found that alprazolam administration did not significantly alter plasma fluphenazine levels.

Are There Distinct Subgroups of Responders and Nonresponders?

Many of the studies reviewed, including our own (Wolkowitz et al. 1988) and a recent open-label study of alprazolam augmentation in schizophrenia (Douyon et al. 1989), have noted a high degree of interindividual variability in response to benzodiazepine augmentation. It is possible that this indicates the presence of distinct subgroups of patients. Evidence presented below supports this possibility. It is unknown if benzodiazepine responsivity represents a "state" (transient) or "trait" (enduring) characteristic of individual patients. The data of Kellner et al. (1975), reviewed here, suggest that some but not all patients who initially respond to benzodiazepine augmentation continue to show favorable responses when readministered the same benzodiazepine.

PREDICTORS OF RESPONSE: BEHAVIORAL AND BIOLOGICAL MARKERS

Many of the studies reviewed found individual patients who responded well to benzodiazepine augmentation. There would be clear advantage in predicting which patients are likely to respond to benzodiazepines, and the further characterization of benzodiazepine responders and nonresponders might yield insights into the pathophysiology of schizophrenic subtypes.

Based on our a priori hypotheses regarding benzodiazepine treatment of schizophrenia, there are several subgrouping variables that are suggested (Table 6-1). Each of these was specifically examined in our initial pilot study (Wolkowitz et al. 1988). Regarding clinical predictors, we found that patients with higher baseline anxiety and psychosis ratings (greater neuroleptic-resistant symptomatology) showed greater alprazolam-associated reductions in Bunney-Hamburg global psychosis ratings. Kahn et al. (1988) observed that schizophrenic patients with panic attacks responded to alprazolam with reductions in positive and negative schizophrenic symptoms as well as panic symptoms. They hypothesized that the presence of panic anxiety may explain the beneficial effects of alprazolam in certain patients. Also, as mentioned earlier, Kellner et al. (1975) similarly found that initial anxiety levels predicted clinical response to neuroleptic augmentation with chlordiazepoxide. It is possible that those patients with more prominent panic or anxiety symptoms respond better to benzodiazepine augmentation. The importance of panic or anxiety in schizophrenic decompensation has been emphasized by Sullivan (1929) and Arieti (1974). It has been estimated that 28–63% of schizophrenic patients experience diagnosable panic attacks (Boyd 1986). It is important, therefore, to determine if this subgroup of patients is particularly amenable to treatment with alprazolam or other benzodiazepines.

We also examined differential effects of alprazolam on dopamine turnover as a possible subgrouping variable. We and others have previously demonstrated that neuroleptics decrease plasma HVA levels in schizophrenic patients in a time-dependent manner (Davis et al. 1985; Pickar et al. 1984, 1986) and that such decreases are significantly correlated in individual patients with reductions in psychosis ratings. Chang et al. (1988) similarly observed distinctly different time-dependent neuroleptic effects on plasma HVA in clinical responders versus nonresponders, with responders showing a decrease in plasma HVA over 5 weeks of neuroleptic treatment and

Table 6-1. Suggested subgrouping variables

Baseline symptomatology ("target symptoms")
Dopamine system responsivity to benzodiazepines
Brain structural or functional differences (especially prefrontal cortex)

---

nonresponders showing an increase or no change. These findings suggest that responders and nonresponders to neuroleptics alone may be differentiated by plasma HVA responses to neuroleptics. In our alprazolam study, we observed no alprazolam-associated group mean changes in plasma HVA levels. When responders were compared to nonresponders, however, a markedly different pattern of plasma HVA response was observed (Figure 6-2).

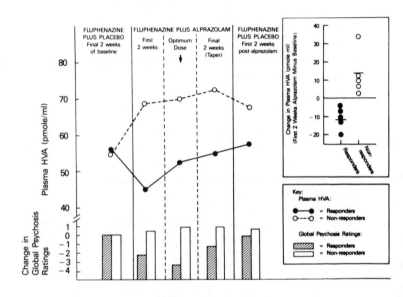

Figure 6-2. *Top*: Change in mean plasma homovanillic acid (HVA) levels associated with alprazolam treatment for responders (*shaded bars* and *solid circles*) and nonresponders (*open bars* and *open circles*), who showed significantly different plasma HVA responses (analysis of variance: group × time [$F = 3.28$, 4/32 df, $P < .05$]). This difference was significant during first 2 weeks of alprazolam treatment ($F = 17.97$, 1/8 df, $P < .02$, corrected for multiple comparisons) and approached significance during optimum-dose alprazolam treatment ($F = 7.71$, 1/8 df, $P < .10$, corrected for multiple comparisons). Considered separately, responders showed significant alprazolam-associated decrease in plasma HVA ($F = 3.56$, 4/16 df, $P < .05$) during first 2 weeks of alprazolam treatment ($P < .05$ by post hoc t test), but not during optimum-dose alprazolam treatment. *Inset*: Maximum separation between responders and nonresponders was seen during first 2 weeks of alprazolam treatment. *Bottom*: Change in global psychosis ratings (compared with baseline) for responders and nonresponders (Wolkowitz et al. 1988).

Whereas nonresponders showed an increase in plasma HVA levels associated with alprazolam treatment, the responders showed a reduction in plasma HVA levels in the first 2 weeks of alprazolam augmentation, with a subsequent partial tolerance to this effect. During the first 2-week period, in which there was the greatest discrimination between responders and nonresponders, there was a complete separation of plasma HVA responses in the five responders compared to the five nonresponders (Figure 6-2). We similarly observed that changes in plasma HVA levels within individual patients were significantly correlated both with changes in Bunney-Hamburg global psychosis ratings and with changes in Abrams and Taylor Rating Scale negative symptom ratings. Alprazolam-associated reductions in plasma HVA levels thus appeared to be a concomitant of therapeutic efficacy with regard to both positive and negative schizophrenic symptoms. Indeed, it is possible that early decreases in plasma HVA levels may predict ultimate clinical outcome, although this will need to be specifically tested in future larger-scale studies. Our observation of partial biochemical tolerance to the alprazolam-associated lowering of plasma HVA levels is intriguing and may be a correlate of the clinical tolerance observed by Csernansky et al. (1988), although, in our study, clinical efficacy was maximal during the weeks following this biochemical tolerance (i.e., the optimum-dose treatment period).

The third subgrouping variable we examined was brain structural changes in the prefrontal cortex. We examined computed tomographic brain scans in all of our patients according to the rating scale developed by Shelton et al. (1988) and modified by Doran et al. (1987). There was no difference in ratings of generalized atrophy or of ventricular-brain ratios between the responders and nonresponders. We found, however, that the clinical responders had significantly greater evidence of prefrontal cortex atrophy than did the nonresponders. The exact significance of this is unclear, but it does implicate the stress/benzodiazepine-sensitive prefrontal cortex in the effects of alprazolam. Our preliminary data raise the possibility that prefrontal cortical atrophy is related to the plasma HVA changes observed in our patients, since those patients with greater evidence of prefrontal cortex atrophy exhibited larger alprazolam-associated reductions in plasma HVA levels. These findings will need to be replicated with a larger sample.

The characterization of patients who *fail* to respond to benzodiazepine augmentation may be as important as the characterization of those who do respond. One example of another modulator of dopaminergic activity is the endogenous opiate system (Janowsky et al. 1983), and we and others (Janowsky et al. 1983;

Pickar et al. 1982) have previously observed responders and nonresponders to acute neuroleptic augmentation with the opiate receptor blocker, naloxone. We have recently had the opportunity to study the chronic effects of the orally active opiate receptor blocker, nalmefene, in several of the schizophrenic patients who had previously failed to respond to alprazolam. Nine such patients (not included in the group of patients described above) were given a double-blind trial of nalmefene added to standard neuroleptics. Five of the nine patients had at least a 30% decrease in their Bunney-Hamburg ratings of psychosis during the nalmefene trial. Two patients with the most impressive decreases in their Bunney-Hamburg ratings of psychosis (54% and 45%, respectively) were not only alprazolam nonresponders but individuals who actually became more psychotic during their double-blind alprazolam trials (20% and 28%, respectively). In both cases, the alprazolam trials had to be prematurely terminated because of these exacerbations in psychosis. This type of dichotomy between a positive response to one augmentation therapy and a negative response to another may be indicative of the importance of different neurotransmitter systems in what may be various subtypes of schizophrenic patients.

CLINICAL CONSIDERATIONS

It is difficult to come away from the review of the literature without concluding that benzodiazepines help some otherwise treatment-resistant patients with schizophrenia. Nevertheless, several clinical caveats are important to highlight. First, only a proportion of schizophrenic patients appear to respond to this intervention. Also, the benefits obtained may be modest and must be weighed against possible risks. Benzodiazepines are potentially addictive, and withdrawal may be problematic (Lader 1983; Mellman and Uhde 1986; Pevnick et al. 1978; Roberts and Vass 1986), especially with high-potency benzodiazepines with short half-lives (e.g., alprazolam). In addition, rebound worsening of symptoms may be seen on withdrawal of the medications (Roberts and Vass 1986; Wolkowitz et al. 1988). Slow tapering of benzodiazepines seems critical in minimizing such reactions. Patients who show poor medication compliance would, therefore, be poor candidates for outpatient treatment with benzodiazepines. Also, some patients exhibit behavioral disinhibition or psychotic exacerbation in response to benzodiazepines; therefore, patients need to be monitored for this eventuality. Stable neuroleptic-responsive outpatients may be at increased risk for such reactions (Dixon et al. 1989). Finally, although several studies suggest initial efficacy of benzodiazepines in some patients, data regarding long-term efficacy (maintenance treatment) are very scanty.

REMAINING QUESTIONS

It is important to emphasize that many of the studies examining benzodiazepine augmentation of neuroleptics, including our own, have employed small sample sizes, and therefore results must be considered preliminary. Several questions remain unanswered:

1. Whether benzodiazepines preferentially affect certain symptoms, such as positive or negative symptoms, anxiety, depression, or extrapyramidal symptoms and akathisia;
2. Whether the beneficial effects of benzodiazepines are transient or sustained;
3. Whether clinical effects are related to plasma benzodiazepine levels;
4. Whether there are clinically significant differences between different benzodiazepines;
5. Whether there is a distinct syndrome of panic anxiety in schizophrenia that predicts good response to alprazolam or other benzodiazepines; and
6. Whether there are biological predictors or concomitants of treatment response.

It is also important to assess further the possibility that biologically distinct subgroups exist relating to benzodiazepine responsivity. Our preliminary data with nalmefene in alprazolam nonresponders provides inferential evidence that psychosis may be due to the complex interplay of a number of different neurotransmitter systems and the importance of different neurotransmitter systems may vary in specific individuals. Schizophrenia, as currently defined, is likely a heterogeneous entity, and any treatment that consistently benefits an identifiable subgroup of otherwise treatment-resistant patients is surely worthwhile pursuing.

REFERENCES

Abrams R, Taylor MA: A rating scale for emotional blunting. Am J Psychiatry 135:226–229, 1978

Altamura AC, Mauri MC, Mantero M, et al: Clonazepam/haloperidol combination therapy in schizophrenia: a double-blind study. Acta Psychiatr Scand 76:702–706, 1987

Arana GW, Ornsteen ML, Kanter F, et al: The use of benzodiazepines for psychotic disorders: a literature review and preliminary clinical findings. Psychopharmacol Bull 22:77–87, 1986

Arieti S: Interpretation of Schizophrenia, 2nd Edition. New York, Basic Books, 1974

Bannon MJ, Roth RH: Pharmacology of mesocortical dopamine neurons. Pharmacol Rev 35:53–68, 1983

Boyd JH: Use of mental health services for the treatment of panic disorder. Am J Psychiatry 143:1569–1574, 1986

Breier A, Schreiber JL, Tarell J, et al: Biological and pharmacologic predictors of outcome. Abstracts of the 140th annual meeting of the American Psychiatric Association, Chicago, IL, 1987a, p 194

Breier A, Wolkowitz OM, Doran AR, et al: Neuroleptic responsivity of negative and positive symptoms in schizophrenia. Am J Psychiatry 144:1549–1555, 1987b

Bunney WE, Hamburg DA: Methods for reliable longitudinal observation of behavior. Arch Gen Psychiatry 9:280–294, 1963

Carlsson A, Lindquist M: Effect of chlorpromazine or haloperidol on formation of 3-methoxytyramine and normetanephrine in mouse brain. Acta Pharmacologica et Toxicologica 20:140, 1963

Chang W, Chen T, Lee C, et al: Plasma homovanillic acid levels and subtyping of schizophrenia. Psychiatry Res 23:239–244, 1988

Creese I, Burt DR, Snyder SH: Dopamine receptor binding predicts clinical and pharmacologic potencies of antischizophrenic drugs. Science 192:481–483, 1976

Csernansky JG, Lombrozo L, Gulevich G, et al: Treatment of negative schizophrenic symptoms with alprazolam: a preliminary open-label study. J Clin Psychopharmacol 4:349–352, 1984

Csernansky JG, Riney SJ, Lombrozo L, et al: Double-blind comparison of alprazolam, diazepam, and placebo for the treatment of negative schizophrenic symptoms. Arch Gen Psychiatry 45:655–659, 1988

Davis JM: Antipsychotic drugs, in Comprehensive Textbook of Psychiatry, Vol 3. Edited by Kaplan HI, Freedman AM, Sadock BJ. Baltimore, MD, Williams & Wilkins, 1980, pp 2257–2289

Davis KL, Davidson M, Mohs RC, et al: Plasma homovanillic acid concentrations and the severity of schizophrenic illness. Science 227:1601–1602, 1985

Dawson GW, Jue SG, Brogden RN: Alprazolam: a review of its pharmacodynamic properties and efficacy in the treatment of anxiety and depression. Drugs 27:132–147, 1984

Deutch AY, Tam SY, Roth RH: Footshock and conditioned stress increase 3,4-dihydroxyphenylacetic acid (DOPAC) in the ventral tegmental area but not substantia nigra. Brain Res 333:143–146, 1985

Dixon L, Weiden PJ, Frances AJ, et al: Alprazolam intolerance in stable schizophrenic outpatients. Psychopharmacol Bull 25:213–214, 1989

Donaldson SR, Gelenberg AJ, Baldessarini RJ: The pharmacologic treatment of schizophrenia: a progress report. Schizophr Bull 9:504–527, 1983

Doran AR, Boroniw J, Weinberger DR: Structural brain pathology in schizophrenia revisited: prefrontal cortex pathology is inversely correlated with CSF levels of homovanillic acid. Neuropsychopharmacology 1:25–32, 1987

Douyon R, Angrist B, Peselow E, et al: Neuroleptic augmentation with alprazolam: clinical effects and pharmacokinetic correlates. Am J Psychiatry 146:231–234, 1989

Guz L, Moraea R, Sartoretto JN: The therapeutic effects of lorazepam in psychotic patients treated with haloperidol: a double-blind study. Current Therapeutic Research, Clinical and Experimental 14:767–774, 1972

Hanlon TE, Ota KY, Agallianos DD, et al: Combined drug treatment of newly hospitalized, acutely ill psychiatric patients. Diseases of the Nervous System 30:104–116, 1969

Hanlon TE, Ota KY, Kurland AA: Comparative effects of fluphenazine, fluphenazine-chlordiazepoxide and fluphenazine-imipramine. Diseases of the Nervous System 31:171–177, 1970

Holden JMC, Itil TM, Keskiner A, et al: Thioridazine and chlordiazepoxide, alone and combined, in the treatment of chronic schizophrenia. Compr Psychiatry 9:633–643, 1968

Janowsky DS, Judd LL, Huey LY, et al: Behavioral effects of opioid receptor antagonists in psychopathologic states. Psychiatr Clin North Am 6:403–414, 1983

Kahn JP, Puertollano MA, Schane MD: Adjunctive alprazolam for schizophrenia with panic anxiety: clinic observation and pathogenetic implications. Am J Psychiatry 145:742–744, 1988

Karson CN, Weinberger DR, Bigelow L, et al: Clonazepam treatment of chronic schizophrenia: negative results in a double-blind, placebo-controlled trial. Am J Psychiatry 139:1627–1628, 1982

Keller HH, Schaffner R, Haefely W: Interaction of benzodiazepines with neuroleptics at central dopamine neurons. Naunyn Schmiedebergs Arch Pharmacol 294:1–7, 1976

Kellner R, Wilson RM, Muldawer MD, et al: Anxiety in schizophrenia: the responses to chlordiazepoxide in an intensive design study. Arch Gen Psychiatry 32:1246–1254, 1975

Lader M: Benzodiazepine withdrawal states, in Benzodiazepines Divided. Edited by Trimble MR. New York, John Wiley, 1983, pp 17–31

Lavielle S, Tassin J, Thierry A, et al: Blockade by benzodiazepines of the selective high increase in dopamine turnover induced by stress in mesocortical dopaminergic neurons of the rat. Brain Res 168:585–594, 1978

Lingjaerde O: Effect of benzodiazepine derivative estazolam in patients with auditory hallucinations: a multicentre double-blind, cross-over study. Acta Psychiatr Scand 65:339–354, 1982

Lingjaerde O: Antipsychotic effect of the benzodiazepines, in Antipsychotics. Edited by Burrows GD, Norman TR, Davies B. Amsterdam, Elsevier Science, 1985, pp 163–172

Lingjaerde O, Engstrand E, Ellingsen P, et al: Antipsychotic effect of diazepam when given in addition to neuroleptics in chronic psychotic patients: a double-blind clinical trial. Current Therapeutic Research, Clinical and Experimental 26:505–514, 1979

Mellman TA, Uhde TW: Withdrawal syndrome with gradual tapering of alprazolam. Am J Psychiatry 143:1464–1466, 1986

Michaux MH, Kurland AA, Agallianos DD: Chlorpromazine-chlordiazepoxide and chlorpromazine-imipramine treatment of newly hospitalized, acutely ill psychiatry patients. Current Therapeutic Research, Clinical and Experimental 8:117–152, 1966

Nestoros JN: Benzodiazepines in schizophrenia: a need for reassessment. Int Pharmacopsychiatr 15:171–179, 1980

Overall JE, Gorham DE: The Brief Psychiatric Rating Scale. Psychol Rep 10:799–812, 1961

Petty F, Kramer GL, Stephenson DMM: Alprazolam blunts the haloperidol-induced increase in dopamine metabolism in frontal neocortex but not caudate: *in vivo* brain microdialysis perfusion. Paper presented at 42nd annual meeting of the Society of Biological Psychiatry, Chicago, IL, 1987

Pevnick JS, Jasinski DR, Haetzen CA: Abrupt withdrawal from therapeutically administered diazepam: report of a case. Arch Gen Psychiatry 35:995–998, 1978

Pickar D: Pharmacotherapeutic approaches to schizophrenia, in Psychopharmacology Consultation. Edited by Jimerson DC, Docherty JP. Washington, DC, American Psychiatric Press, 1986, pp 71–103

Pickar D: Perspectives on a time-dependent model of neuroleptic action. Schizophr Bull 14:255–268, 1988

Pickar D, Vartanian F, Bunney WE Jr, et al: Short-term naloxone administration in schizophrenic and manic patients. Arch Gen Psychiatry 39:313–319, 1982

Pickar D, Labarca R, Linnoila M, et al: Neuroleptic-induced decrease in plasma homovanillic acid and antipsychotic activity in schizophrenic patients. Science 225:954–957, 1984

Pickar D, Labarca R, Doran AR, et al: Longitudinal measurement of plasma homovanillic acid levels in schizophrenic patients. Arch Gen Psychiatry 43:669–676, 1986

Pickar D, Wolkowitz OM, Doran AR, et al: Clinical and biochemical effects of verapamil administration to schizophrenic patients. Arch Gen Psychiatry 44:113–118, 1987

Roberts K, Vass N: Schneiderian first-rank symptoms caused by benzodiazepine withdrawal. Br J Psychiatry 148:593–594, 1986

Roth RH: Neuroleptics: functional chemistry, in Neuroleptics: Neurochemical, Behavioral and Clinical Perspectives. Edited by Coyle JT, Enna SJ. New York, Raven, 1983, pp 119–156

Salzman C: Use of benzodiazepines to control disruptive behavior in inpatients. J Clin Psychiatry 49:13–15, 1988

Salzman C, Green A, Rodriguez-Villa F, et al: Benzodiazepines combined with neuroleptics for management of severe disruptive behavior. Psychosomatics 27:17–21, 1986

Shelton RC, Karson CN, Doran AR, et al: Cerebral structural pathology in schizophrenia: evidence for a selective prefrontal cortical defect. Am J Psychiatry 145:154–163, 1988

Singhal RL, Rastogi RB, Lapierre YD: Diazepam potentiates the effect of neuroleptics on behavioral activity as well as dopamine and norepinephrine turnover: do benzodiazepines have antipsychotic potency? J Neural Transm 56:127–138, 1983

Sullivan HS: Research in schizophrenia. Am J Psychiatry 9:553–567, 1929

Tam SY, Roth RH: Selective increases in dopamine metabolism in the prefrontal cortex by the angiogenic beta-carboline FG-7142. Biochem Pharmacol 34:1595–1598, 1985

Torrey EF: Schizophrenia and Civilization. Northvale, NJ, Jason Aronson, 1980

Wolkowitz OM, Pickar D, Doran AR, et al: Combination alprazolam-neuroleptic treatment of the positive and negative symptoms of schizophrenia. Am J Psychiatry 143:85–87, 1986

Wolkowitz OM, Breier A, Doran A, et al: Alprazolam augmentation of the antipsychotic effects of fluphenazine in schizophrenic patients. Arch Gen Psychiatry 45:664–671, 1988

Wolkowitz OM, Reus VI, Breier A, et al: Alprazolam-neuroleptic treatment in schizophrenia. Schizophrenia Research 2:215, 1989

Wood PL: Actions of GABAergic agents on dopamine metabolism in the nigrostriatal pathway of the rat. J Pharmacol Exp Ther 222:674–679, 1982

Chapter 7

Lithium and Carbamazepine Augmentation in Treatment-Refractory Schizophrenia

S. Charles Schulz, M.D.
E. Michael Kahn, M.D.
Robert W. Baker, M.D.
Robert R. Conley, M.D.

Chapter 7

Lithium and Carbamazepine Augmentation in Treatment-Refractory Schizophrenia

The theme of this volume is the treatment of patients with schizophrenia who are not fully responsive to neuroleptic treatment. In the introduction, a discussion of the significance of this problem was begun, including the prevalence of patients who are poorly responsive and some of the factors that may be associated with less-than-optimal response.

In addition to the studies described in the introduction, there are data from the treatment strategies in schizophrenia study being conducted as a multicenter investigation that would indicate that the prevalence of poor response may be more significant than was previously imagined. In this study, in which three dosing strategies of maintenance neuroleptic treatment and their interaction with two types of family therapy are examined, nearly 40% of the subjects who begin the trial are unable to be stabilized within 6 months (Keith et al. 1990). Furthermore, a significant group of subjects are not able to sustain their initial improvement over the 2-year duration of the study, indicating that early initial response is not always maintained. The importance of this study, and its estimate of the problem of poor response, is that nearly 300 patients from five sites have been studied, and the criteria for stabilization are not overly strict. This leads us to believe that using the figures from the early placebo-controlled studies (Cole et al. 1964, 1966) alone may underestimate the prevalence of poor responders.

Another factor in understanding the significance of poor response to neuroleptic treatment is the long-term impact of poor response. A study by Brier et al. (1987) showed that the most robust predictor of global outcome (e.g., symptoms, work, and social interactions) was with neuroleptic response during treatment on the ward. If this finding is generalizable, it could mean that neuroleptic response is associated with other good prognostic signs. However, it could also mean that good outcome is related to the effectiveness of the agents used to treat psychosis and is not inexorably linked to demographic poor prognosis factors.

We have been concerned about the fate of the poorly responsive patient for a number of years. We have observed that the usual course for a schizophrenic patient who did not have appreciable reduction of symptoms with neuroleptics was to be transferred to the state system for further inpatient treatment. Therefore, pharmacologic regimens to reduce psychotic symptoms were sought. After a survey of the literature, we concluded that the greatest amount of evidence for effective augmenting treatments were for lithium and carbamazepine. In this chapter, a comprehensive and critical review of the augmenting trials with lithium and carbamazepine will be presented. Even though there are numerous articles that are supportive of the use of these augmenting agents, not all of the studies were designed to consider the issue that is central to this volume: the treatment of nonresponsive patients. Special attention will be paid to this issue throughout the review. Then a description of our pilot study of a blind trial of adding lithium or carbamazepine will be presented.

LITHIUM AUGMENTATION

Most articles that discuss the use of lithium begin by acknowledging Cade's (1949) article on the treatment of mania and schizophrenia. Of interest is that lithium appears to have been recognized as an agent for treatment of agitation even in the 19th century (Hammond 1871).

Interest in the use of lithium for schizophrenia, especially in the United States, was renewed when the drug was allowed to be used in 1969. However, the earliest studies (Johnson et al. 1968; Prien et al. 1972; Shopsin et al. 1971), in which patients with schizoaffective disorder were studied, not only cast doubt on the use of lithium for schizophrenic patients, but introduced data that indicated that lithium might actually lead to worsening in schizophrenia. Only Prien et al. carefully dissected the different hypotheses about how lithium might be useful and what a successful trial might mean. They showed that, for mildly as opposed to highly agitated patients, lithium was as effective as neuroleptic treatment. At about the same time, Cohen and Cohen (1974) reported that there were a number of patients who suffered an irreversible brain syndrome following the use of combined lithium and haloperidol. Although treatment of bipolar patients frequently involved the use of a combination of antipsychotic medications and lithium carbonate, it is our opinion that the Cohen and Cohen report delayed exploration of the use of combined lithium and neuroleptics for schizophrenic patients.

Small et al. (1975) were the first to have conducted a trial of lithium as an augmenting agent for schizophrenic patients who were unresponsive to regular neuroleptic treatment. In this study, 22 patients were entered in an A-B-A-B (A = lithium, B = placebo) addition to neuroleptics. The patients were well characterized as nonresponsive; 81% were classified as having premorbid asociality. In addition, to address the concerns initiated by the earlier Johnson et al. (1968) and Shopsin et al. (1971) articles, neuropsychological testing was done throughout the study to assess whether or not lithium led to a confusional state.

The results of this study were very encouraging. Of the 22 patients who entered the study, nearly half were continued on lithium based on their favorable response. In addition, seven patients were discharged from the inpatient state hospital unit. The authors of this study noted that there was a decrease in global illness as well as in excitement as assessed on the Brief Psychiatric Rating Scale (BPRS) (Overall and Gorham 1962). In our opinion, one of the findings that has provided continued enthusiasm for lithium studies in schizophrenia is that there was improvement in manifest psychosis, social competence, and personal neatness. These results indicated that the addition of lithium was more than just added sedation or the treatment of unrecognized affective symptoms. This study also showed that, for the patients who were tested, there was not a general confusional state produced by the combination of drugs.

The next study to be published was that by Growe et al. (1979) (Table 7-1). This study reported on the results of eight patients with schizophrenia who were judged to be unresponsive to neuroleptic treatment. Six of the eight were schizophrenic; the other two were schizoaffective. The design of this study was similar to the Small et al. (1975) study in that it included two periods of lithium and two of placebo. The results were reported as a comparison of the period when lithium was in the therapeutic range versus when it was not. No categorical (e.g., number of responders) data were presented, and the only variable that showed a significant diminution during the lithium period was psychotic excitement. Therefore, Growe et al. concluded that when lithium was used to augment neuroleptics in schizophrenic patients, its effect was through the decrease in symptoms related to mania.

Table 7-1. Lithium and neuroleptics in the treatment of schizophrenia

Reference	Subjects	Design	Results			Comments
			N responders	Symptoms		
Small et al. (1975)	• 4 male; 18 female • Age = 36 • Chronic schizophrenia; 8 schizoaffective (4 manic; 4 depressed). • 81% probable or definitive premorbid asociality. • All were neuroleptic treatment failures.	• Random assignment to one of two sequences: A-B-A-B; B-A-B-A (A = lithium; B = placebo). • Above sequence added to stable neuroleptic regimen.	• 15 subjects completed entire trial. • 10/20 were continued on lithium. • 7 discharged from chronic care.	• Improvement in global illness, mannerisms and posturing, cooperation, excitement (BPRS). • Improvement in social competence, personal neatness, irritability, manifest psychosis.		• One patient dropped from study due to memory loss and confusion. • Responders were older and in hospital longer. • Subtype of schizophrenia did not influence outcome.
Biederman et al. (1979)	• 25 male; 11 female • Age = approximately 31 • Consecutive admission of psychotic patients with excitement.	• Haloperidol begun on admission. • Lithium or placebo started at same time. • Doses of both drugs adjusted	• Not reported.	• Total BPRS score lower at 5 weeks in lithium group. • Global Clinical Impression slightly better in lithium group.		• One patient with lithium toxicity. • Positive effects seen in symptoms other than mania. • Authors note

Study	Sample	Design		Findings	Comments
	• RDC schizo-affective. • 18 with more than 2 hospitalizations. • 18 without drug treatment in prior 2 weeks.	by clinical needs.		• No difference in mania scale for the two groups. • Affective; schizoaffectives improve more than schizophrenic affectives. • Less depression in lithium group.	• study simulates clinical situation. • Note patients not previous nonresponders.
Growe et al. (1979)	• 8 male/female • Age = 25 • 6 schizophrenic; 2 schizoaffective (RDC). • Failed previous neuroleptic treatment.	• 16-week study with 4-week epochs. • A-B-A-B (A = lithium; B = placebo). • Neuroleptic kept stable. • Analysis compared lithium in therapeutic range to below range.	• Not reported.	• Only symptom reduced by lithium was psychotic excitement.	• No lithium toxicity. • Authors suggest added lithium's effect only on symptoms related to mania.

Table 7-1. Lithium and neuroleptics in the treatment of schizophrenia (continued)

Reference	Subjects	Design	Results		Comments
			N responders	Symptoms	
Carman et al. (1981)	• 10 male; 8 female • Age = 22-62 • 11 schizophrenic; 7 schizoaffective (RDC) • None ever married. • All schizoid premorbid or intermorbid. • Intermittent or continuous hospitalization for mean 13.1 years.	• 8 weeks stabilized on neuroleptics. • 12-week study with 4-week epochs. • Two sequences; A-B-A; B-A-B (A = lithium; B = placebo). • Patients rated by nurses (inpatient Behavioral Rating Scale). Scales of psychosis, depression, and arousal.	• 10 significantly better on arousal. • 5 significantly better on psychosis. • 5 significantly better on depression (5 worsened).	• Notes primary effect may have been in mania, with thought disorders secondary.	• 4 dramatic lithium responders had neuroleptic withdrawn. 3 had relapses supporting synergistic action. • No neurotoxic reactions. • Episodic course or affective symptoms favored added lithium response. • Suggest lithium trial in nonresponsive patients.

Note.   BPRS = Brief Psychiatric Rating Scale; RDC = Research Diagnostic Criteria.

The study that included the most patients, that by Biederman et al. (1979), was not designed to address the specific problem of the persistently psychotic schizophrenic patient. By design, this trial included 36 consecutive admissions who met the criteria of "psychotic excitement" and were diagnosed as schizoaffective by Research Diagnostic Criteria (Spitzer et al. 1978). Unlike in the Growe et al. (1979) study, not all of the patients were neuroleptic unresponsive, although 18 of the patients had been in the hospital twice previously. The patients were started on haloperidol in the hospital and then randomly assigned to added lithium or placebo. Both the haloperidol and lithium were adjusted according to clinical needs. For this group of patients, lithium proved to be significantly better as judged by the total BPRS score at the fifth week of the study. It should be noted that both the placebo and lithium augmentation groups improved during the study, as would be expected by the design of the trial. Looking at the type of improvement seen in this study, Biederman et al. noted that there were no differences in changes in mania between the placebo and lithium groups, but did note less depression in the lithium-augmented patients. As in the Small et al. (1975) study, the authors noted changes in symptoms other than mania and felt that, because their study simulated a usual clinical situation, lithium could be useful in treating patients with schizoaffective disorder who have "psychotic excitement."

The question of the unresponsive patient was again addressed by Carman et al. (1981) at St. Elizabeths Hospital of the National Institute of Mental Health in Washington, D.C. The 18 patients studied in this report appear to have been chronic nonresponders similar to those discussed in the Kane et al. (1988) article on clozapine. The patients evaluated in this placebo-controlled lithium augmentation trial consisted of 11 schizophrenic patients and 7 patients with schizoaffective disorder. None had been married, and all were characterized as having schizoid premorbid functioning. Following 8 weeks of stabilization on neuroleptics, patients were begun on a 12-week trial period with an A-B-A or B-A-B (A = lithium, B = placebo) design, where each epoch lasted 4 weeks. Categorically, there were 10 patients who were judged to be significantly better in the area of arousal. Five were judged better on psychosis, and five improved in the ratings of depression. Concerning the question of the relation of manic symptoms and changes in psychotic symptoms in schizophrenic patients, Carman et al. noted that all the patients who had a decrease in psychosis ratings also had a decrease in mania, thus bringing into question again the mechanism of lithium's beneficial factors in schizophrenia. This study was the first to assess the question of whether or not lithium and neuroleptics acted through a synergistic mechanism, by removing neuroleptics in four of the successfully treated patients. Three of the patients who had improved with the added lithium had a rapid return of their symptoms when the neuroleptic was discontinued, indicating that the improvement was due to both drugs, not just the response to lithium alone. The point about the synergism of action of lithium and neuroleptic is underscored by a case report by Bigelow et al. (1981), in which a patient was blindly assessed with both drugs over a number of months and always did better with both agents.

In summary, there are four placebo-controlled trials that assess the usefulness of adding lithium to neuroleptics in patients with schizophrenia or schizoaffective disorder. All are in a positive direction, although two are only mildly so. To our knowledge, there is not a negative trial of lithium combined with neuroleptics for schizophrenia or affective disorders. Even though all the investigators address the lithium-neuroleptic subject, only three for a total of 48 patients approach the question of lithium for nonresponsive patients. In the two that give a proportion of the responders (Carman et al. 1981; Small et al. 1975), the rate of response ranges from approximately 47% down to 28%. Even so, the authors of the reports suggest its usefulness in the clinical arena.

The question about which types of symptoms are most affected still seems to be largely unanswered. Although Small et al. (1975) demonstrated a decrease in schizophrenia symptoms, Growe et al. (1979) did not see such a response. The Biederman et al. (1979) study indicated that global illness and the total BPRS were significantly decreased, but it should be remembered that the subjects were patients with schizoaffective disorder who were further classified as having "psychotic excitement" at entry to the study. Even though the Carman et al. (1981) article shows that 5 of the 18 patients who were studied had a significant decrease in psychosis, inspection of their table of results reveals that all who had a decrease in psychosis also had a decrease in mania. For clinicians, the point may be moot, as the major goal is to relieve suffering. In this case, the addition to lithium carbonate is better than placebo in each trial. Also, the Carman et al. article does provide evidence that the effect is secondary to a synergistic effect, indicating that both drugs are needed. In our opinion, further work along these lines is indicated. For the investigator, the mechanism of action of lithium's ability to decrease some symptoms is intriguing and could lead to further studies that might pinpoint what lithium does to reduce global ratings scores.

We have had experience in using lithium carbonate as an augmenting drug for unresponsive patients in a number of settings (e.g., university hospitals, private and state hospital facilities). In our opinion, the use of lithium carbonate in unresponsive patients is a generally safe strategy (Baastrup et al. 1976), and we encourage a trial of lithium for those who have not had a satisfactory response to usual treatment because, for approximately one-fourth to one-half of patients, the addition can mean a difference in the placement after discharge. Most clinicians are aware of the concerns about using neuroleptic combined with lithium and are aware of monitoring of lithium levels and for signs of neuromuscular irritability (Prakash et al. 1982a, 1982b). Recent reports have pointed out that such neuromuscular or central nervous system effects are more likely to occur with higher doses of neuroleptics. Also, as can be seen from the Cohen and Cohen (1974) article, high serum levels of lithium (e.g., 1.5–2.4) are not advisable. Interestingly, many patients who have lithium added to neuroleptic not only improve, but seem to have a decreased need for neuroleptic.

CARBAMAZEPINE AUGMENTATION

A number of different avenues of evidence have converged to suggest that carbamazepine may be useful for patients with schizophrenia. The first is that, as carbamazepine became more widely used as an anticonvulsant, it was recognized that there were changes in patient's psychiatric symptoms that did not appear to be similar to those seen when other anticonvulsants were used. This led investigators, mostly neurologists, to consider the psychotropic properties of the drug. Closer to schizophrenia research, Dalby (1971) observed in the mid-1970s that patients with psychosis secondary to temporal lobe epilepsy did well when carbamazepine was used. These connections to the temporal lobe and symptoms of psychosis led Stevens et al. (1979) to investigate the use of carbamazepine in patients diagnosed as schizophrenic who also had temporal lobe electroencephalogram (EEG) abnormalities as assessed by telemetry EEG. Although the patients so treated did not make significant improvement, the idea of using carbamazepine in schizophrenic patients with EEG abnormalities did not stop there.

Although the thrust of this volume has been the unresponsive patient, usually defined as a person with persistent psychosis, patients with psychosis who are violent despite every attempt at treatment with neuroleptics have attracted attention of investigators. One of the studies described further in this chapter (Hakola and Lauluma 1982) is illustrative of the approach of adding carbamazepine to neuroleptics in patients with schizophrenia who have abnormal EEGs and violent behavior (Table 7-2). A different group of studies also promoted enthusiasm for the use of carbamazepine in treatment-refractory schizophrenic subjects. Okuma et al. (1973) demonstrated the usefulness of carbamazepine for manic-depressive disorder, a finding that was extended in the United States by Ballenger and Post (1980); patients who have been refractory to lithium treatment seem to be the patients who are most responsive to carbamazepine. Also, in the laboratory, Post and colleagues (Post 1977; Post et al. 1976) have linked the observations of carbamazepine's effectiveness with the "kindling" hypothesis, which may also apply to certain cases of unresponsive psychosis.

The logical step to determine the potential for carbamazepine in schizophrenia in the late 1970s was to identify patients who might have psychosis and EEG abnormalities and to assess the impact of the anticonvulsant. In an elegant experiment, Stevens et al. (1979) identified schizophrenic patients with EEG abnormalities by EEG telemetry and then examined the effect of adding carbamazepine to neuroleptic on behavior ratings. In the two patients in whom carbamazepine was tried, worsening was seen in both. It is possible that this report dampened enthusiasm for carbamazepine for some time; it was 3 years before another published report appeared.

The first study to report an open clinical trial of the addition of carbamazepine to neuroleptics in schizophrenic patients was that of Hakola and Lauluma (1982). Their study focused on schizophrenic women with abnormal EEGs and frequent violent outbursts. The patients had been tried on neuroleptics up to "high" doses (mean, 2,040 chlorpromazine equivalents). The authors reported that violent behavior and symptoms of psychosis were decreased when carbamazepine was introduced. The degree of response could not be assessed because no rating scales were used, but the overall outcome in a patient population that is difficult to treat provided new enthusiasm for the use of carbamazepine.

Neppe (1983) described a clinical trial of carbamazepine in a group of psychiatric patients who were not epileptic, but who had EEG abnormalities; 9 of the 13 patients were receiving neuroleptics. All subjects received carbamazepine and placebo in a double-blind, crossover study. Of the 11 completers, 9 were reported as improved (a statistically significant proportion). However, Neppe noted that no BPRS cluster nor the total BPRS scores were different on carbamazepine compared to the placebo period. Thus the first two reports in the 1980s showed some advantage for a subset of schizophrenic patients who were hypothesized to benefit from an

Table 7-2. Carbamazepine and neuroleptics in the treatment of schizophrenia

Reference	Subjects	Design	Results			Comments
			N responders	Symptoms		
Hakola and Lauluma (1982)	• Schizophrenic women with violent outbursts. • Age = 38.5 • All had abnormal EEGs. • Hospital stay = 9.8 years	• Patients all tried on high-dose neuroleptics (2,040 mg/day CPZ equivalents). • Carbamazepine added at mean dose of 600 mg/day for mean 2.7 years. • Open study.	• Violent behavior or nearly disappeared in 4/8. • 4/8 had decrease in schizophrenic symptoms.	• No ratings mentioned.		• An early pilot study of note. • Pharmacokinetic interactions may play a role.
Neppe (1983)	• 13 male/female • Age = 18–59 • "Non-epileptic, chronic patients" with temporal lobe abnormality in EEG. • 10 schizophrenic. • 9 received concomitant neuroleptics.	• Double-blind, randomized, within-patient comparison of carbamazepine versus placebo (3 week baseline; 6 weeks each carbamazepine or placebo.	• 9/11 improved, 1/11 same, 1/11 better on placebo ($P = .02$).	• Carbamazepine better than placebo on overall and global ratings, but not total BPRS. • No BPRS cluster different between carbamazepine versus placebo. • EEG deteriorated in 6 patients.		• Kinetic interactions unknown. • May be useful in "nonresponsive" patients.

Table 7-2. Carbamazepine and neuroleptics in the treatment of schizophrenia (continued)

Reference	Subjects	Design	Results			Comments
			N responders	Symptoms		
Klein et al. (1984)	• 19 male; 24 female • Age = approximately 33 • Diagnosed as "excited psychosis." • Generally no prior response to lithium.	• Double-blind, placebo-controlled study of carbamazepine versus placebo added to haloperidol (about 40 mg/day).	• Not reported.	• Total BPRS significantly better for carbamazepine group. • Improvement apparent in schizophrenic and affective symptoms.		• Study included large amount of lithium and/or neuroleptic nonresponders. • 10 patients crossed over after double-blind did well on carbamazepine.
Kidron et al. (1985)	• 8 male; 3 female • Age = 42 • Hospitalized = 15 years.	• Double-blind, placebo-controlled trial of carbamazepine versus placebo randomized crossover. • 5 weeks of each treatment. • Carbamazepine and haloperidol levels measured.	• None improved enough to consider continuing carbamazepine.	• Total BPRS no different between carbamazepine and placebo.		• Basically report of lowered haloperidol levels during carbamazepine augmentation.

| Herrera et al. (1987) | • 6 male
• Age = 39.8
• DSM-III schizophrenia.
• Chronic nonresponders rigorously defined.
• Ill a mean of 14 years. | • Single-blind assessment of added carbamazepine to neuroleptic (average 1,980 mg/day CPZ 15).
• Trial lasted 10 weeks. | • No specific criteria for responder.
• One dramatic clinical improver.
• Two significantly better on carbamazepine. | • Significant improvement in depression, anxiety, and withdrawal.
• No significant improvement in thought disorder. | • One patient discharged because of reactive hepatitis.
• Question whether change in withdrawal secondary to decreased neuroleptic level. |
| Ballenger and Post (1984) | • 3 male; 3 female
• Schizophrenic.
• EEG: normal, 1; abnormal, 5 | • Case reports of carbamazepine alone or with neuroleptics. | • All 6 showed improvement in behavior. | • Decrease in "spells" of agitation and belligerence.
• Decrease in psychosis. | • Target group for carbamazepine may be those patients with aggressive outbursts and abnormal EEGs. |

Table 7-2. Carbamazepine and neuroleptics in the treatment of schizophrenia (continued)

Reference	Subjects	Design	Results			Comments
			N responders	Symptoms		
Luchins (1984) [Study 1]	• 7 patients: 6 schizophrenia 1 personality disorder. • Age = 34.5 • Hospitalization = 11.6 years. • Normal EEG. • All violent histories.	• Chart review. • 6 weeks neuroleptic alone. • 6 weeks neuroleptic plus carbamazepine. • 6 weeks neuroleptic alone.	• 6/7 had fewer violent episodes.	• Significantly fewer aggressive episodes. • Decrease in verbal hostility.		• Early study to show benefits for patients with normal EEGs.
Luchins (1984) [Study 2]	• 19 patients: 15 schizophrenia 1 organic delusional disorder 1 personality disorder 1 mild retardation 1 organic personality disorder.	• Same as above except no 3rd period off carbamazepine.	• Not reported.	• Decrease in frequency of aggressive episodes. • Decrease in verbal hostility.		• No difference in effect of carbamazepine on EEG normal versus abnormal.

Study	Subjects	Methods	Side Effects	Results	Comments
	• Age = 36 • Hospitalization = 11.0 years. • Normal and abnormal EEG.				
Dose et al. (1987)	• 9 male; 13 female • Age = 26.5 • ICD schizophrenia or schizoaffective. • No EEG abnormal.	• Double-blind, placebo-controlled study of added carbamazepine for 4 weeks. • Patients all on haloperidol 6 mg/day at start of augmentation trial. • 1-week washout at end of 4-week trial.	• Not reported.	• Both carbamazepine and placebo groups made significant improvement on BPRS and IMPS. • Significant difference between neuroleptic requirement; carbamazepine group needed less drug.	• May be a useful adjunct to reduce neuroleptic dose.

Note. EEG = electroencephalogram; CPZ = chlorpromazine; BPRS = Brief Psychiatric Rating Scale; ICD = International Classification of Diseases; IMPS = Inpatient Multidimensional Rating Scale anticonvulsant: those with violent outbursts and those with abnormal EEGs.

Carbamazepine's broader use was indicated by the next trial, that of Klein et al. (1984). Consecutive admissions of psychotic patients who were characterized by excitement were randomly assigned to receive carbamazepine or placebo added to haloperidol (mean dose, approximately 40 mg/day). Although the study was not designed to address the problem of nonresponders specifically, many of the patients had prior failures to neuroleptic and/or lithium treatment. The results demonstrated that by 5 weeks the total BPRS score was lower for the carbamazepine adjunctive group compared to placebo. The investigators also noted that improvement was seen in both schizophrenic and affective symptoms. This study shows that carbamazepine may be useful in this group of psychotic patients, but the design may have actually diminished the chance of showing an advantage for the added drug by not allowing for prior stabilization on neuroleptic, as the placebo added to neuroleptic group showed a diminution in symptoms during the treatment period as they improved on neuroleptic.

The questions about the role of violent behavior and/or EEG abnormalities as they pertained to carbamazepine as an augmenting agent to neuroleptics were addressed by two articles in the *Psychopharmacology Bulletin* in 1984. In the first article, Luchins (1984) described two chart reviews (studies 1 and 2) performed at a state hospital. Seven patients with violent outbursts, but normal EEGs—in contrast to the Hakola and Lauluma (1982) and Neppe (1983) studies—received carbamazepine for at least 6 weeks, and 6 of the 7 patients were noted to have decreased violent episodes. This was the first study to show a potential advantage for the use of added carbamazepine in patients who were selected for normal EEGs. In study 2, 19 more patients who were predominantly schizophrenic were given augmenting carbamazepine. In this second group, some patients had normal EEGs while others did not. Again, there was a decrease in aggressive episodes, and successful treatment was not associated with either normal or abnormal EEG.

In the second article, Ballenger and Post (1984) used a case report format to describe their experience with carbamazepine in patients with schizophrenia. Five of the six patients had abnormal EEGs. Some patients received carbamazepine added to neuroleptics; others received carbamazepine alone. All six patients were rated as improved globally, with specific decreases in "spells" of agitation as well as a decrease in psychosis. The authors suggested that a target group of schizophrenic patients who could benefit from carbamazepine treatment are those with EEG abnormalities and episodic violent outbursts.

The first study to explore blood levels of both carbamazepine and neuroleptic (haloperidol) was an important negative report. Kidron et al. (1985) performed a double-blind, placebo-controlled, crossover study that did not demonstrate a difference between added carbamazepine or placebo. What this group did show was that the addition of carbamazepine to haloperidol led to a significant decrease in haloperidol levels. A subsequent study (Jann et al. 1985) and a study by our group (Kahn et al. 1990) have confirmed this phenomenon, although the extent of neuroleptic blood level lowering and its clinical correlates are not well established.

The next carbamazepine augmenting article (Dose et al. 1987) is hard to understand in light of the Kidron et al. (1985) article, but is noteworthy because it is well controlled and discusses the interesting possibility that the regular dose of neuroleptic can be dropped when an augmenting drug is used. The subjects in this study were all diagnosed as schizophrenic and had no EEG abnormalities. All subjects were on haloperidol (6 mg at the start of the study), and both the added placebo and carbamazepine groups improved. However, the group that received added carbamazepine needed statistically less neuroleptic. The authors concluded that the augmenting drug may reduce the neuroleptic requirement, but this is hard to understand in light of the Kidron et al. article, which showed carbamazepine to lower neuroleptic levels. For studies that tested carbamazepine as an adjunct to high-dose neuroleptic regimens, one could theorize that decreasing neuroleptic levels could lead to transient improvement in some cases, but it is hard to see how this would occur with an already low dose unless the general sedating properties of carbamazepine were helpful to the patients.

Perhaps the most seriously and persistently ill patients to be tested with added carbamazepine were reported on by Herrera et al. (1987). This group selected patients similar to those who participated in the clozapine study (Kane et al. 1988). Of the six patients who participated, there was one clear responder; as a group, the patients were less anxious, depressed, and withdrawn. There was no statistically significant change in psychotic symptoms, although they were reduced. This trial may indicate that, for the chronically ill group (ill a mean of 14 years), not selected because of symptoms of excitement, the impact of carbamazepine may not be great.

A LITHIUM VERSUS CARBAMAZEPINE AUGMENTATION TRIAL

Whereas many of the trials of lithium and carbamazepine added to neuroleptics were focused on patients with target symptoms such as "excited psychosis" or "violent outbursts," few of the reports described above addressed the general issue of the nonresponsive patient. In an attempt to examine the potential augmenting role for these drugs in schizophrenic patients who were persistently psychotic, our group designed a study that included a specific definition for response, demographic and biological characterization of patients, and then a double-blind trial of lithium versus carbamazepine in nonresponders to acute treatment.

To identify responders and nonresponders to neuroleptic treatment prospectively, a 4-week haloperidol treatment trial was administered to 61 consecutively admitted patients who were diagnosed as schizophrenic or schizoaffective by DSM-III (American Psychiatric Association 1980) criteria. The patients received a 5 mg/bid starting dose of haloperidol and were assessed at baseline plus weekly with BPRS. During the 4-week treatment with haloperidol, total haloperidol levels (haloperidol and reduced haloperidol) were measured each week by radioimmunoassay, which provided results in 24 hours, allowing an adjustment of haloperidol dose to bring haloperidol level into a therapeutic range. The 4-week neuroleptic trial was completed by 44 patients.

For the purpose of this study, a relatively high therapeutic range was selected; we did not wish to have a patient characterized as a nonresponder because of an inadequate dose of neuroleptic (Van Putten, Chapter 5, this volume). Rather than define response as a percentage of decrease in symptoms, a BPRS score of 40 or below and positive symptoms of psychosis were used to identify responders. (For this study, the BPRS of Bigelow and Murphy [unpublished], which has 24 items, was used.) This definition was selected because, even though a patient may have some reduction in symptoms with neuroleptic treatment, there is a need for treatment of persistent psychosis. Seventeen patients were classified as nonresponders to acute haloperidol treatment and 14 received blinded capsules containing either lithium carbonate or carbamazepine in addition to continued haloperidol treatment. Doses of the augmenting drugs were adjusted by a research coordinator to achieve therapeutic levels. The added medicine trial lasted for 2 weeks. Haloperidol level assessments were continued during the added medicine portion of the trial, and haloperidol dose could be changed if the level was outside the therapeutic range. Physician and nurse raters were blind to the added medication and continued to complete BPRS and global rating scales.

During the 4-week neuroleptic trial, those patients who were considered unresponsive did have a significant decrease in total BPRS ratings, but as a group had no change in ratings between week 3 and 4. As has been previously noted by us (Schulz et al. 1989), the nonresponders were characterized by higher scores on a battery of neurologic soft signs and lower scores on the Mini-Mental Status Exam (Folstein et al. 1975), which would indicate that the nonresponders had slightly more "organicity" than responders. However, the means ($\pm$ SD) of the ventricular brain ratio of the responders (6.01 $\pm$ 2.0) and nonresponders (6.4 $\pm$ 3.24) were essentially the same.

When the ratings at the end of haloperidol treatment of all the patients who received added medicine were compared to the endpoint ratings, there was a significant reduction in symptoms as assessed by total BPRS score (56.7 $\pm$ 14.5 to 43.5 $\pm$ 9.5, t = 2.92, P = .012) and the BPRS thought disorder factor (12.2 $\pm$ 4.2 to 8.9 $\pm$ 3.11, t = 3.42, P = .005). Of the 14 patients who received augmenting drugs, 8 were assigned to lithium, and 5 met criteria for response after the 2 weeks of augmentation; of the 6 assigned to carbamazepine, 2 met the criteria of responders. Total BPRS scores were reduced for both groups: from 58.8 $\pm$ 18.7 to 41.1 $\pm$ 7.42 (t = 2.45, P = .044) for those who received lithium and from 53.8 $\pm$ 6.5 to 46.7 $\pm$ 11.7 (t = 2.00, P = .102) for those who received carbamazepine. The thought disorder factor, a measure of psychotic symptoms, was also reduced during treatment with both drugs: for lithium from 11.6 $\pm$ 4.6 to 7.6 $\pm$ 2.6 (t = 2.57, P = .037) and for carbamazepine from 13.2 $\pm$ 3.8 to 10.8 $\pm$ 3.0 (t = 3.54, P = .024). Although there were more patients who responded to lithium carbonate, there was not a statistical difference between the two augmenting treatments. Both drugs were well tolerated, and no patient had to stop treatment because of side effects.

One of the aims of the study was to determine correlates of change with added medication. Demographically, compared with the nonresponders, the seven patients who responded to either augmenting treatment were ill for a briefer period of time (3.1 versus 14.5 years, P < .10) and had higher Mini-Mental Status Exam scores on admission to the study (27.4 versus 23.5, P < .10); more of them tended to have a family history of schizophrenia (5 versus 1, P < .10). One serendipitous finding in our study, which is consistent with Kidron et al. (1985), was the effect of added carbamazepine on serum haloperidol concentrations, which we have reported separately (Kahn et al. 1990). Because haloperidol blood levels were monitored with rapid turnaround, haloperidol dose could be increased to keep levels in therapeutic range.

In summary, our study utilized a prospective and objective means to identify acute nonresponse to neuroleptic treatment and then compared the effects of added lithium or carbamazepine. We concluded that the added medicines were useful based on the improvement of patients during their use and that there had been no change in symptoms in the week prior to the augmentation. Furthermore, a number of the patients who had neurologic soft signs and enlarged ventricles improved with augmentation treatment, which can be interpreted as a hopeful sign for patients who previously may not have received vigorous treatment. However, because of the lack of a placebo group during the augmentation period, an assessment of how much of the change was due to the added medicine or was secondary to the patient's or rater's expectation of change cannot be determined.

CONCLUSIONS

After an era in which there were few empirical data to support nonneuroleptic augmentation to antipsychotic treatment for schizophrenia, many agents have been tested. The medications that have received the most attention in this regard are lithium carbonate and carbamazepine, and the trials and anecdotal experiences of both drugs have been summarized and reviewed in this chapter. Despite the number of trials and the probable extensive use of these drugs added to neuroleptics, the rationale of their use for nonresponsive patients is far from clear.

For lithium carbonate, although there are the four controlled augmentation trials (Biederman et al. 1979; Carman et al. 1981; Growe et al. 1979; Small et al. 1975), not all were designed to address the question of its utility as an agent to help previously unresponsive patients. The Small et al. study is the most compelling because it utilized chronically ill patients and the group noted that 7 of 15 completers of the protocol were able to leave the hospital, thus indicating a clinically significant, not just statistically significant, advantage. The Carman et al. study and our pilot work presented in this chapter also support a role for lithium in the nonresponder subtype. A contribution of our study is the demonstration of the utility of lithium carbonate to decrease total BPRS scores and symptoms of psychosis, as judged by the thought disorder factor, in the acute care setting. All things considered however, it must be remembered that only 48 patients have been tested in controlled conditions.

Another question that is frequently discussed about the use of added lithium for the treatment of unresponsive psychosis is whether added lithium is synergistic with neuroleptics or whether patients are responding to lithium alone. Although the Small et al. (1975) and Growe et al. (1979) studies used A-B-A-B designs to investigate added lithium, only in the Carman et al. (1981) study was the neuroleptic discontinued. The rapid relapse of three-fourths of the subjects certainly suggests synergism. A case report by Bigelow et al. (1981), in which a woman with schizoaffective disorder was tried and failed on lithium alone after responding to lithium and neuroleptic, also supports the synergism concept.

Lastly, there is the question of whether the global improvement with lithium carbonate is secondary to decreasing the psychosis characteristic of schizophrenia or a decrease in affective disorder symptoms. The Small et al. (1975) study and ours would indicate that symptoms of psychosis are reduced when lithium is added. In our study, neither mania nor depression were changed, but neither were high when augmenting drugs were added. Although the Carman et al. (1981) study did note a decrease in psychosis ratings during the period of added lithium, it was invariably accompanied by a decrease in ratings of mania. In the Biederman et al. (1979) study, in which lithium plus haloperidol was better than haloperidol plus placebo, all the subjects were selected for having schizoaffective disorder.

The same sorts of questions can be asked about the data supporting the use of carbamazepine added to neuroleptics for nonresponders. Unlike lithium added to neuroleptics, the early articles on the addition of carbamazepine to neuroleptics focused on specific subtypes of schizophrenia (e.g., patients with schizophrenia who were still violent despite neuroleptic treatment). Therefore, although there are more articles reviewed in this chapter about carbamazepine than lithium, not as many address the general schizophrenic patient whose psychosis is unresponsive to neuroleptic treatment.

Looking first at the evidence that added carbamazepine might help unresponsive patients, one notes there are not many reports that address the issue and that most are not strong. The Kidron et al. (1985) study was actually the first to address nonresponders not selected for the treatment of violence, abnormal EEG, or epilepsy. In their group of 11 subjects, none improved enough to be considered for further treatment with carbamazepine. An important part of the study was the description of dramatically lowered haloperidol blood levels following added carbamazepine. This finding has since been replicated by other groups (Jann et al. 1985), and it appears that this interaction has important clinical and research implications. The

Herrera et al. (1987) article examined six rigorously identified non-responders and found one who improved dramatically. In their added carbamazepine study, Dose et al. (1987) reported that both the carbamazepine and placebo groups improved at the same rate. The carbamazepine group needed less neuroleptic, which is puzzling in light of the pharmacokinetic articles. Our results are equally lukewarm in that two-sixths meet criteria for response. A significant aspect of our strategy was that if the haloperidol level dropped during the added carbamazepine segment of the trial (which it did), then the haloperidol dose could be adjusted upward. It seems, therefore, that added carbamazepine may be of mild help for the unselected non-responder.

For the selected nonresponder (e.g., a neuroleptic-treated patient who is still violent), the case for carbamazepine is stronger. The results of the studies assessing violent or aggressive behavior both point in this direction. This may even extend to the "excited" psychosis patient, as reported by Klein et al. (1984), although the design was not chosen to address previously unresponsive patients. In the other selected patient category are those patients with abnormal EEGs or an epileptic picture. Neppe (1983) demonstrated usefulness of added carbamazepine in patients with temporal lobe abnormality on EEG. Ballenger and Post (1984) reported similar findings.

Therefore, it appears there is continued promise for the use of carbamazepine in some schizophrenic patients whose target symptoms have been demonstrated to be reduced by its addition to neuroleptic. At this time, the utility for the general nonresponder is not as certain. However, further studies need to attend to the pharmacokinetic issues raised by recent studies.

The points raised by this review and discussion lead to the question of whether these drugs have a place in the clinical arena. It appears there are significant data to suggest that a patient can be tried on augmenting lithium and that improvement will occur in a substantial number. Although the combination does not lead to neuropathic changes as often as suggested by Cohen and Cohen (1974), close observation for neuromuscular symptoms and monitoring of blood levels is important (Prakash et al. 1982a, 1982b). At present, there is no indication of a pharmacokinetic interaction between lithium and neuroleptics. For carbamazepine, the evidence for the selected patients seems good enough to warrant its use for them. Neppe (1988) wrote an informative article describing how to use carbamazepine clinically. We feel it is very important that neuroleptic blood levels be monitored when carbamazepine is used in this way.

In summary, the evidence for augmenting neuroleptic regimen

with either lithium or carbamazepine has been reviewed and discussed. There is sufficient evidence, in our opinion, for its use in the treatment of schizophrenia, but we also feel further research is needed. In addition, there is enough evidence for efficacy for these drugs to be used in further research as pharmacologic probes into the nature of the unresponsive patient.

REFERENCES

American Psychiatric Association: Diagnostic and Statistical Manual of Mental Disorders, 3rd Edition. Washington, DC, American Psychiatric Association, 1980

Baastrup PC, Hoffnagel P, Sorensen R, et al: Adverse reactions in treatment with lithium carbonate and haloperidol. JAMA 236:2645–2646, 1976

Ballenger JC, Post RM: Carbamazepine in manic-depressive illness: a new treatment. Am J Psychiatry 137:782, 1980

Ballenger JC, Post RM: Carbamazepine and neuroleptics in the treatment of schizophrenia. Psychopharmacol Bull 20:572–584, 1984

Biederman J, Lerner Y, Belmaker RH: Combination of lithium carbonate and haloperidol in schizoaffective disorder: a controlled study. Arch Gen Psychiatry 36:327–333, 1979

Bigelow LB, Weinberger DR, Wyatt RJ: Synergism of combined lithium-neuroleptic therapy: a double-blind placebo-controlled case study. Am J Psychiatry 138:81–83, 1981

Brier AF, Schreiber JL, Tarell J, et al: Biological and pharmacological predictors of outcome. Paper presented at the annual meeting of the American Psychiatric Association, Chicago, IL, May 14, 1987

Cade JFJ: Lithium salts in the treatment of psychotic excitement. Med J Aust 36:3–49, 1949

Carman J, Bigelow LB, Wyatt RH: Lithium combined with neuroleptics in chronic schizophrenic and schizoaffective patients. J Clin Psychiatry 42:124–128, 1981

Cohen WJ, Cohen NH: Lithium carbonate, haloperidol, and irreversible brain damage, JAMA 230:1283–1287, 1974

Cole JO, Goldberg SC, Klerman GL: Phenothiazine treatment in acute schizophrenia. Arch Gen Psychiatry 10:246–261, 1964

Cole JO, Goldberg SC, David JM: Drugs in the treatment of psychosis: controlled studies, in Psychiatric Drugs. Edited by Solomon P. New York, Grune & Stratton, 1966, pp 153–180

Dalby MA: Antiepileptic and psychotropic effect of carbamazepine

(Tegretol) in the treatment of psychomotor epilepsy. Epilepsia 12:325–334, 1971

Dose M, Apelt S, Emrich HM: Carbamazepine as an adjunct of antipsychotic therapy. Psychiatry Res 22:303–310, 1987

Folstein MF, Folstein SE, McHugh PR: Mini-Mental State: a practical method for grading the cognitive state of patients for the clinician. J Psychiatr Res 12:189–198, 1975

Growe GA, Crayton JA, Klass DB: Lithium in chronic schizophrenia. Am J Psychiatry 136:454–455, 1979

Hakola HPA, Lauluma VA: Carbamazepine in treatment of violent schizophrenics. Lancet 1:1358, 1982

Hammond WA: A Treatise on Diseases of the Nervous System. New York, Appleton & Company, 1871

Hererra JM, Sramek JJ, Costa JF: Efficacy of adjunctive carbamazepine in the treatment of chronic schizophrenia. Drug Intell Clin Pharm 21:355–358, 1987

Jann MW, Ereshefsky L, Saklad SR, et al: Effects of carbamazepine on plasma haloperidol levels. J Clin Psychopharmacol 5:106–108, 1985

Johnson G, Gershon S, Hekimian LJ: Controlled evaluation of lithium and chlorpromazine in the treatment of manic states: an interim report. Compr Psychiatry 9:563–573, 1968

Kahn EM, Schulz SC, Perel JM, et al: Change in haloperidol level due to carbamazepine: a complicating medication for schizophrenia. J Clin Psychopharmacol 10:54–57, 1990

Kane J, Honigfeld G, Singer J, et al: Clozaril collaborative study group: clozapine for the treatment-resistant schizophrenic: a double-blind comparison with chlorpromazine. Arch Gen Psychiatry 45:789–796, 1988

Keith SJ, Matthews SM, Schooler NR: Psychosocial Treatment of Schizophrenia: A Review of Psychoeducational Family Approaches in Schizophrenia Research. Edited by Tamminga CA, Schulz SC. New York, Raven, 1990

Kessler Z: Carbamazepine for psychotropic disorders. Hosp Formul 18:207–215, 1983

Kidron R, Averbuch I, Klein E, et al: Carbamazepine-induced reduction of blood levels of haloperidol in chronic schizophrenia. Biol Psychiatry 20:219–222, 1985

Klein E, Beutal E, Lerer B, et al: Carbamazepine and haloperidol versus placebo and haloperidol in excieted psychosis: a controlled study. Arch Gen Psychiatry 41:165–170, 1984

Luchins B: Carbamazepine and neuroleptics in the treatment of schizophrenia. Psychopharmacol Bull 20:569–571, 1984

Neppe VM: Carbamazepine as adjunctive treatment in nonepileptic chronic inpatients with EEG temporal lobe abnormalities. J Clin Psychiatry 44:326–330, 1983

Neppe VM: Carbamazepine in nonresponsive psychosis. J Clin Psychiatry 49:22–28, 1988

Okuma T, Kishimoto A, Inoue K, et al: Anti-manic and prophylactic effects of carbamazepine on manic-depressive psychosis. Folia Psychiatr Neurol Jpn 27:283–297, 1973

Overall JE, Gorham DR: The Brief Psychiatric Rating Scale. Psychol Rep 10:799–812, 1962

Post RM: Clinical implications of a cocaine-kindling model of psychosis, in Clinical Neuropharmacology, Vol 2. Edited by Klawans HL. New York, Raven, 1977, pp 777–816

Post RM, Kopanda RT: Cocaine, kindling, and psychosis. Am J Psychiatry 133:627–634, 1976

Prakash R, Kelwala S, Ban TA: Neurotoxicity in patients with schizophrenia during lithium therapy. Compr Psychiatry 23:271–273, 1982a

Prakash R, Kelwala S, Ban TA: Neurotoxicity with combined administration of lithium and a neuroleptic. Compr Psychiatry 23:567–571, 1982b

Prien RF, Caffey EM, Klett CJ: A comparison of lithium carbonate and chlorpromazine in the treatment of excited schizo-affectives. Arch Gen Psychiatry 27:182–189, 1972

Schulz SC, Conley RR, Kahn EM, et al: Nonresponders to neuroleptics: a distinct subtype, in Schizophrenia: Scientific Progress. Edited by Schulz SC, Tamminga CA. New York, Oxford University Press, 1989, pp 341–350

Shopsin B, Kim SS, Gershon S: A controlled study of lithium vs. chlorpromazine in acute schizophrenics. Br J Psychiatry 119:435–440, 1971

Small JG, Kellans JJ, Milstein V, et al: A placebo-controlled study of lithium combined with neuroleptics in chronic schizophrenic patients. Am J Psychiatry 132:1315–1317, 1975

Spitzer RL, Endicott J, Robins E: Research Diagnostic Criteria: rationale and reliability. Arch Gen Psychiatry 35:773–782, 1978

Stevens JR, Bigelow L, Denney D, et al: Telemetered EEG-EOG during psychotic behaviors of schizophrenia. Arch Gen Psychiatry 36:251–269, 1979

Chapter 8

Presynaptic Modulators of Dopamine Synthesis in the Treatment of Chronic Schizophrenia

Jeffrey L. Berlant, M.D., Ph.D.

Chapter 8

Presynaptic Modulators of Dopamine Synthesis in the Treatment of Chronic Schizophrenia

The conventional psychopharmacologic treatment of chronic schizophrenia consists of administration of neuroleptic medications. Therapeutic programs built on the assumption that neuroleptic medications are sufficient strategies for meeting the medication needs of patients, however, fail to come to grips with the substantial subpopulation of neuroleptic-refractory patients. Drug response studies suggest that approximately 30% of patients with chronic schizophrenia show minimal if any improvement in psychotic symptoms (Davis et al. 1982). The existence of this subgroup warrants ongoing investigation into new pharmacologic strategies. The purpose of the following review is to revive interest in an old biochemical hypothesis that has not received adequate scientific evaluation but that could lead to better treatments for refractory schizophrenia.

Neuroleptic-refractory schizophrenic patients raise both theoretical and practical problems. Why do these patients fail to respond to potent dopamine-blocking agents if the biochemical pathophysiology of schizophrenia is linked to an aberration in dopamine activity? Perhaps certain pathophysiologic mechanisms for the production of schizophrenic symptoms cannot be subsumed under the dopamine hypothesis but are due to other as yet poorly identified causes. Perhaps some patients with hyperdopaminergic psychoses respond poorly to neuroleptics because of biochemical or hormonal factors that either block the action of neuroleptics on dopamine receptors or neutralize the effects of dopamine blockade.

One approach for analyzing this theoretical problem as well as for generating potentially new psychopharmacologic approaches is reduction of presynaptic dopaminergic activity either as an alternative or as a supplement to postsynaptic blockade. Through intervention at one or more levels of the dopamine synthetic pathway, reduction in hyperdopaminergic activity and psychotic symptoms may be possible when symptoms do not respond to postsynaptic blockade alone.

A small number of clinical investigators have attempted treatment of schizophrenia with novel strategies employing pharmacologic agents that influence presynaptic dopaminergic activity. In the following section, I will review the synthesis, storage, and release of dopamine; examine the findings of clinical trials of presynaptic dopaminergic interventions in chronic schizophrenia; and propose areas in which future clinical research efforts might return rewards.

DOPAMINE SYNTHESIS, STORAGE, AND RELEASE

Intraneuronal dopamine is formed via the conversion of tyrosine to dihydroxyphenylalanine (DOPA) by tyrosine hydroxylase, which constitutes the rate-limiting step in dopamine formation. DOPA is decarboxylated into dopamine and stored in intraneuronal granules awaiting future release. Dopamine-containing granules empty into the synaptic cleft under the influence of bioelectric neuronal signals modulated through the action of a negative feedback system of inhibitory presynaptic dopamine receptors (dopamine autoreceptors) (Carlsson 1975). Neuropharmacologic interventions at each level of this synthetic pathway have been clinically investigated (Figure 8-1).

TYROSINE HYDROXYLASE INHIBITORS

The prototypical drug that blocks tyrosine hydroxylase is alpha-methyl-p-tyrosine, generally known as metyrosine. This medication is currently marketed for the treatment of pheochromocytoma, but it has been used in the treatment of schizophrenia (Table 8-1). The two small uncontrolled studies that have been conducted (both including samples of chronic schizophrenic populations) using treatment with metyrosine alone failed to suggest any positive effect (Charalampous and Brown 1967; Gershon et al. 1967). When neuroleptics were combined with metyrosine, some but not all open trials suggested an improvement in symptoms (Carlsson et al. 1972, 1973; Larsson et al. 1984), and three of four small controlled studies suggested a significant superiority of metyrosine over placebo (Carlsson 1978; Magelund et al. 1979b; Nasrallah et al. 1977; Walinder et al. 1976).

Carlsson (1978) examined the effect of metyrosine on cerebrospinal fluid (CSF) homovanillic acid (HVA) levels to ascertain whether a change in dopamine activity had occurred as part of the medication's effect. All of the patients who demonstrated a marked reduction in CSF HVA (5/6) were responders, which provides some independent evidence of inhibition of dopamine synthesis. The absence of nonresponders in this study, however, and the presence of response in one patient whose baseline HVA was low suggest that a different study design is needed to understand this relationship.

INHIBITORS OF DOPAMINE INTRAGRANULAR STORAGE

The prototypical agent for reduction or depletion of intragranular stores of dopamine and several other neurotransmitters is reserpine. Reserpine, an alkaloid of the snakeroot plant, *Rauwolfia serpentina*, is a widely used antihypertensive. The snakeroot plant had been used as an ancient Vedic herbal remedy for psychosis; the active alkaloid reserpine was identified in 1952 (Barsa and Kline 1955, 1956).

Initial studies by Barsa and Kline (1955, 1956) of the use of reserpine for the treatment of psychosis were followed in the 1950s by more than 20 randomized controlled trials that demonstrated the

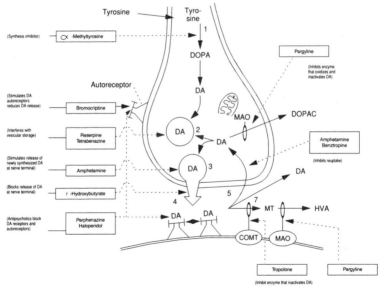

Figure 8-1. Biosynthetic pathway and presynaptic modulatory mechanisms for dopamine. DA = dopamine; DOPA = dihydroxyphenylalanine; DOPAC = dihydroxyphenylacetic acid; HVA = homovanillic acid; MAO = monoamine oxidase; COMT = catechol-O-methyl transferase; MT = methyldopamine. Adapted from Kandel and Schwartz 1985 with permission from Elsevier Science Publishing, and adapted from Cooper et al. 1986 with permission from Oxford University Press.

antipsychotic efficacy of this agent (Berlant 1986). Used alone, oral or intramuscular therapeutic doses varied from 0.5–15 mg/day. Reserpine is the only presynaptic modulator of dopamine activity that has received an indication from the United States Food and Drug Administration for the treatment of psychosis.

Reserpine therapy produced three treatment response phases. Ini-

Table 8-1.   Clinical trials in schizophrenia with metyrosine (alpha-methyl-p-tyrosine)

Reference	N	Diagnosis	Dosage (g/day)	Design	Results
Neuroleptic-free					
Open trials					
Gershon et al.					
(1967)	8	AS	.6–3		2 better, 2 worse
	5	CS			1 better, 2 worse
Charalampous and Brown					
(1967)	17	CS	2		no improvement
With neuroleptics					
Open trials					
Carlsson et al.					
(1972)	5	CS	2		3/5 better
Carlsson et al.					
(1973)	6	CS	2		6/6 better
Larsson et al.					
(1984)	4	CS	2		no change
Controlled trials					
Walinder et al.					
(1976)	4	CS	2	random	metyrosine > placebo
Carlsson					
(1978)	8	RCS	2	crossover	metyrosine > placebo
Nasrallah et al.					
(1977)	10	RCS	3	random	metyrosine = placebo
Magelund et al.					
(1979a)	12	CS	2.75	crossover	metyrosine = haloperidol both > placebo

Note.   AS = acute schizophrenia; CS = chronic schizophrenia; RCS = refractory chronic schizophrenia.

tial "sedation" was often followed by a "turbulent" phase, in which psychotic symptoms of agitation, hallucinations, and delusions increased, presumably due to an initial release of dopamine into the synaptic cleft. If the patient could be carried through this phase, after a number of weeks an "integration" phase could be observed, during which the symptoms of psychosis remitted. Barsa and Kline (1955) observed that 50 mg of chlorpromazine blocked the turbulent phase and brought attention to the neuroleptic as a "potentiator" of reserpine. Four comparative studies of chlorpromazine versus chlorpromazine with reserpine during the 1950s, however, failed to demonstrate any consistent superior advantage to the combination regimen but did note an overall increase in troublesome side effects (Barsa and Kline 1956; Hollister et al. 1955; Kinross-Wright 1955; Tuteur and Lepson 1957). By 1960, reserpine had fallen out of favor following the advent of the neuroleptics during the second half of the 1950s. The nail was hammered on the coffin lid for reserpine in 1962 when a large Veterans Administration hospital study comparing seven neuroleptics to reserpine and placebo demonstrated that despite reserpine's superiority to placebo, all the neuroleptics exceeded the antipsychotic efficacy of reserpine (Lasky et al. 1962).

The concept that reserpine might be useful in combination with neuroleptics for treatment-refractory schizophrenia (Table 8-2) appeared in a study that found that 11 of 14 treatment-refractory schizophrenic patients responded to reserpine when chlorpromazine had failed (Kinross-Wright 1955). Little further work was done with reserpine in schizophrenia until Bacher and Lewis (1978) reported possible synergism between reserpine and neuroleptics for treatment-refractory schizophrenic outpatients. Berlant (1986) reported a nearly identical response rate of 50% in 1986 in a group of treatment-resistant psychotic patients in a residential treatment setting.

The Berlant (1986) study examined response to the addition of reserpine to a neuroleptic or to a neuroleptic with lithium in 36 patients with chronic psychosis (18 male, 18 female) with a mean age of 32 years (range, 20–68). The mean duration of continuous illness

Table 8-2. Clinical trials in schizophrenia with reserpine

Reference	N	Diagnosis	Results
With neuroleptics			
Open trials			
Kinross-Wright (1955)	14	RCS	11 improved (79%)
Bacher and Lewis (1978)	25	RCS	12 improved (48%)
Berlant (1986)	36	RCS	18 improved (50%)

Note. RCS = refractory chronic schizophrenia.

was 11 years (range, 5–18). Diagnoses according to DSM-III (American Psychiatric Association 1980) criteria as assigned by a psychiatric rater included undifferentiated schizophrenia, 10; paranoid schizophrenia, 2; schizoaffective disorder, 15; bipolar disorder, manic, with psychotic features, 4; and atypical psychosis, 4. Patients considered for reserpine therapy displayed persistent, severe psychotic symptoms, such as delusions, auditory hallucinations, derailment, and intense agitation. Their functional capacity was severely impaired, which required their placement in a locked residential facility. They were unable to perform sufficiently well to allow transfer to a halfway house setting. The length of stay in the facility varied from weeks to months, and some patients had been unable to leave the facility until they were treated with reserpine. Previous treatment with a series of multiple neuroleptics had resulted in minimal response. Treatment for a minimum of 3 weeks with lithium carbonate with serum levels of 1.2 mEq/L or higher and a neuroleptic had occurred without apparent improvement. Several patients had received additional pharmacologic trials including antidepressants and carbamazepine without appreciable benefit.

Reserpine treatment consisted of the addition of reserpine to preexisting medications. Dosage range varied from 0.5–6.0 mg/day, with most patients receiving 1.5–3.5 mg/day. Reserpine doses were usually increased in 0.25-mg bid increments every week until the patient either improved or developed intolerable adverse effects. Subsequent to doing this study, I have found that attempts to increase the dosage more rapidly have resulted in termination of the trial because of sudden agitation, sometimes with violent behavior uncharacteristic of the patients' previous symptoms. Excessively rapid dosage increases may trigger a turbulent phase; therefore, weekly increases are probably prudent.

Psychosis ratings were retrospectively assigned based on a scale of 1 = no evidence of psychosis, 2 = mildly psychotic, 3 = moderately psychotic, and 4 = extremely psychotic. Ratings were assigned following examination of the medical record, interviews with treatment staff, interviews with attending psychiatrists, and direct observation of the patients by myself during the study period. Overall, 18 of 36 patients (50%) improved to a clinically significant extent. When responders were compared to nonresponders, there was negligible change in scores for both groups over the 4-week period prior to initiation of reserpine, but the mean score for responders dropped to 1.6 compared to 3.1 for nonresponders (Figure 8-2).

Areas of clinical improvement included both positive and negative schizophrenic symptoms, blunted affect, inhibited activity, social isolation, and task performance. Some of the responders were able to attend occupational therapy groups and other activities despite inability to attend prior to the administration of reserpine.

Age, duration of illness, concomitant prescription of lithium, and psychiatric diagnosis were nonpredictors of clinical response to reserpine. Factors that appeared to be clinical predictors of response included sex (females 67%, males 33%); the presence of delusions, agitation, or affective lability; and a history of prior exposure to phencyclidine. Adverse effects included frequent excessive salivation, parkinsonism, and gastrointestinal distress. Approximately 10% developed depressive symptoms, which resulted in termination of the reserpine trial. Five patients were removed within 1 week because of an apparent turbulent psychotic reaction following the introduction of reserpine.

INHIBITORS OF DOPAMINE RELEASE FROM INTRANEURONAL GRANULES

A prototypical inhibitor of intragranular dopamine release is gamma-hydroxybutyrate (GHB), a chemical analogue of gamma-amino-butyric acid (GABA). This simple organic acid is used medically outside the United States as an anesthetic agent.

Using GHB in refractory chronic schizophrenic patients, Tanaka et al. (1966) found improvement in some subgroups. Unfortunately, evaluation of this study is difficult because of omission of a critical

RESERPINE RESPONSE

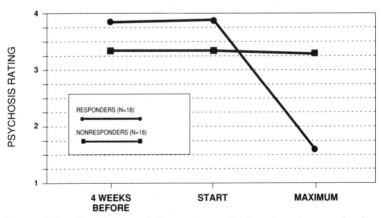

Figure 8-2. Comparison of changes in psychosis ratings (see text for details) before and after addition of reserpine in reserpine responders versus nonresponders.

descriptive table from the publication. Of the 48 chronic schizophrenic patients refractory to neuroleptics treated with GHB, the number treated concomitantly with neuroleptics is unstated. Response rates were overall high: five of seven hebephrenic patients, five of eight "atypical" patients, "60%" (of an unstated denominator) of catatonic patients, but only two of eight patients with "positive symptoms." One would not have expected from the dopamine hypothesis of schizophrenia that patients with the positive symptoms, presumably associated with elevated dopaminergic activity, would do worst.

A subsequent controlled study using GHB alone found no superiority over placebo (Schulz et al. 1981); the subjects in this sample may have been more neuroleptic responsive than those in the Tanaka et al. (1966) study. This study also compared CSF HVA levels in GHB responders versus nonresponders and found a significantly higher level in responders at baseline, with striking separation between values in each group. Whether CSF HVA is a predictor of response to dopamine release inhibitors such as GHB warrants much more study.

A controlled study of GHB in combination with neuroleptics found no advantage over placebo (Levy et al. 1983); however, the small size of the sample ($N = 10$) precludes rejection of the possibility that GHB has active antipsychotic properties, at least in a subpopulation of patients (Table 8-3).

Table 8-3. Clinical trials in schizophrenia with gamma-hydroxybutyrate

Reference	N	Diagnosis	Dosage (g/day)	Design	Results
Neuroleptic-free					
Open trials					
Tanaka et al. (1966)	48	RCS	1–8		hebephrenic 5/7 improved catatonic 60% improved positive symptom 2/6 improved atypical 5/6 improved
Controlled trials					
Schulz et al. (1981)	7	CS	8–16	crossover	2 better, 3 worse
With neuroleptics					
Controlled trials					
Levy et al. (1983)	10	CS	12	crossover	GHB = placebo

Note GHB = gamma-hydroxybutyrate; RCS = refractory chronic schizophrenia; CS = chronic schizophrenia.

DOPAMINE AUTORECEPTOR AGONISTS

A number of drugs function as dopamine agonists—for example, bromocriptine, apomorphine, levodopa, and piribedil. These compounds are of theoretical interest because of their capacity to stimulate presynaptic receptors for dopamine. Presynaptic dopamine receptors are potent feedback inhibitors of presynaptic dopamine release that play a far greater role in the regulation of dopamine release than do postsynaptic receptors. The potential effect of dopamine agonists is to reduce synaptic dopamine activity by diminishing presynaptic release of dopamine and thereby reduce psychotic symptomatology.

The prototypical agent is bromocriptine, an ergot alkaloid. Bromocriptine is a standard treatment for parkinsonism because of its dopamine agonist properties. At low concentrations it is a presynaptic agonist; at high concentrations it is also a postsynaptic agonist. Potentially, high-dose bromocriptine might function as a psychotogenic agent, but low-dose bromocriptine might function as an antipsychotic (Meltzer et al. 1983). Unfortunately, the dosage at which the crossover in dopamine subpopulation activity in humans occurs is not precisely known.

Four open clinical trials of bromocriptine alone conducted in small numbers of schizophrenic patients (Table 8-4) provide little indica-

Table 8-4. Clinical trials in schizophrenia with bromocriptine

Reference	N	Diagnosis	Dosage (mg/day)	Design	Results
Neuroleptic-free					
Open trials					
Trabucchi et al. (1977)	12	CS	15/37.5		no improvement
King (1978)	2	CS	60		1 worse
Brambilla et al. (1983)	10	CS	40		no change
Meltzer et al. (1983)	7	CS	.25–6		transiently improved
	2	SA	.5		1 better
Controlled trials					
Tamminga and Schaffer (1979)	7	CS	10	crossover	3 worse
With neuroleptics					
Controlled trials					
Cutler et al. (1984)	11	RCS	2	random	bromocriptine > placebo

Note. CS = chronic schizophrenia; SA = schizoaffective disorder; RCS = refractory chronic schizophrenia.

tion of antipsychotic efficacy (Brambilla et al. 1983; King 1978; Meltzer et al. 1983; Trabucchi et al. 1977). Most of the doses employed (0.25–60 mg) may have been excessively high to have a selectively presynaptic effect, and the study population did not target neuroleptic-nonresponsive patients. Whether lower doses or a different population might prove more effective remains to be studied. A single controlled study of seven subjects actually found placebo superior to bromocriptine (Tamminga and Schaffer 1979); the study dose of 10 mg may well have been in the psychotogenic range.

The only study in neurolepticized patients (Cutler et al. 1984), using a 2-mg single-dose design, found bromocriptine superior to placebo over several ensuing hours. The reason for this apparent therapeutic effect is unclear: it could be ascribed to a selective presynaptic effect of the 2-mg dose, the use of a neuroleptic-refractory population, the short duration of comparison, or symptomatic improvement because of acute reductions in akathisia and other parkinsonian side effects of neuroleptics that have been associated with worsening of psychotic symptoms in some patients (Van Putten et al. 1974). The observation requires further investigation in more extended studies.

CONCLUSIONS

Despite the theoretical importance of a strategy of decreasing presynaptic dopamine activity for the treatment of chronic psychosis, relatively little work has been done with presynaptic dopamine modulators. Overall, the most dramatic antipsychotic effect has been seen with reserpine, both with and without concomitant use of neuroleptics.

None of the studies suggests that any of these presynaptic modulators are equal, let alone superior, to conventional neuroleptics for treatment-responsive patients. These preparations do not appear likely to supplant neuroleptics as primary treatment for schizophrenia. They may, however, have value as augmenting agents for the treatment of neuroleptic-refractory patients.

Metyrosine may be helpful for augmentation of the antipsychotic effect of neuroleptics in both refractory and drug-responsive schizophrenia. It is relatively low in toxicity in standard doses and warrants further investigation.

GHB, whether used alone or with neuroleptics, appears ineffective for unselected patients with schizophrenia. It may have some utility in neuroleptic-refractory patients. Because of the dated nature of the largest treatment study, this agent requires systematic investigation starting from scratch. The work by Schulz et al. (1981) suggests that use of potential biological predictors such as HVA may help to select GHB responders. The use of such parameters should be included in any future work.

Bromocriptine alone appears ineffective for unselected schizophrenic patients who are free of neuroleptics. It too may be useful as an augmenting agent for neuroleptics in neuroleptic-refractory patients. The current evidence for this statement is limited to a brief period of improvement following a single dose of bromocriptine. Further investigation in the refractory subpopulation is warranted, however, both on the basis of this preliminary work and on theoretical considerations, using well-designed dose-response curves to isolate selective presynaptic effects.

Reserpine, with a nearly consistent record of positive responses in multiple open trials conducted in neuroleptic-refractory patients, warrants a randomized clinical trial of reserpine augmentation of neuroleptics in refractory schizophrenia. The magnitude of the response is great enough in empirical studies to justify its current use in treatment-resistant patients, for whom so little other hope exists. A randomized clinical trial would be welcome, however, to confirm the validity of the open trials and to complete the data base for its efficacy prior to widespread reintroduction of this medication.

Since certain subtypes of refractory schizophrenia may not be associated with dopaminergic overactivity, a proper test of the efficacy of these presynaptic dopamine modulators should be conducted associating drug response to dopamine activity status. Biological correlates of dopamine overactivity, such as CSF or plasma HVA, may predict presynaptic modulator responsivity, as in the Schulz et al. (1981) study using GHB, and should be included routinely in future studies.

Finally, clinical investigators should give consideration to the possibility of applying principles of combination chemotherapy to treatment-refractory patients. The presynaptic modulators work on multiple points in the dopamine synthetic pathway. An additive effect of their simultaneous use may occur. Should we not think of joining the use of metyrosine with reserpine, low-dose bromocriptine, and a GABA-ergic drug? Perhaps one day psychiatrists will join our colleagues in oncology by employing combination chemotherapy for the treatment of our most difficult and hopeless patients.

REFERENCES

American Psychiatric Association: Diagnostic and Statistical Manual of Mental Disorders, 3rd Edition. Washington, DC, American Psychiatric Association, 1980

Bacher NM, Lewis HA: Addition of reserpine to antipsychotic medication in refractory chronic schizophrenic outpatients. Am J Psychiatry 135:488–489, 1978

Barsa JA, Kline NS: Combined reserpine-chlorpromazine in treatment of disturbed psychotics. AMA Archives of Neurology and Psychiatry 74:280–286, 1955

Barsa JA, Kline NS: A comparative study of reserpine, chlorpromazine in treatment of disturbed psychotics. AMA Archives of Neurology and Psychiatry 76:90–97, 1956

Berlant JL: Neuroleptics and reserpine in refractory psychoses. J Clin Psychopharmacol 6:180–184, 1986

Brambilla F, Scarone S, Pugnetti, et al: Bromocriptine therapy in chronic schizophrenia: effects on symptomatology, sleep patterns, and prolactin response to stimulation. Psychiatry Res 8:159–169, 1983

Carlsson A: Dopaminergic autoreceptors, in Chemical Tools in Catecholamine Research, Vol 2. Edited by Almgren O, Carlsson A, Engel J. Amsterdam, North-Holland, 1975, pp 219–229

Carlsson A: Does dopamine have a role in schizophrenia? Biol Psychiatry 13:3–21, 1978

Carlsson A, Persson T, Roos B-E, et al: Potentiation of phenothiazines by alpha-methyltyrosine in treatment of chronic schizophrenia. J Neural Transm 33:83–90, 1972

Carlsson A, Roos B-E, Walinder J, et al: Further studies on the mechanism of antipsychotic action: potentiation by alpha-methyltyrosine of thioridazine effects in chronic schizophrenics. J Neural Transm 34:125–132, 1973

Charalampous KD, Brown S: A clinical trial of alpha-methyl-para-tyrosine in mentally ill patients. Psychopharmacologia (Berlin) 11:422–429, 1967

Cooper, JR, Bloom FE, Roth RH: The Biochemical Basis of Neuropharmacology, 4th Edition. New York, Oxford University Press, 1986, p 202

Cutler NR, Jeste DV, Kaufmann CA, et al: Low dose bromocriptine: a study of acute effects in chronic medicated schizophrenics. Prog Neuropsychopharmacol Biol Psychiatry 8:277–283, 1984

Davis JM, Janicak P, Chang S, et al: Recent advances in the pharmacologic treatment of the schizophrenic disorders, in Psychiatry 1982: The American Psychiatric Association Annual Review, Vol 1. Edited by Grinspoon L. Washington, DC, American Psychiatric Press, 1982, pp 178–228

Frye PE, Pariser SF, Kim MH, et al: Bromocriptine associated with symptoms exacerbation during neuroleptic treatment of schizoaffective schizophrenia. J Clin Psychiatry 43:252–253, 1982

Gershon S, Hekimian LJ, Floyd A, et al: Alpha-methyl-p-tyrosine (AMT) in schizophrenia. Psychopharmacologia (Berlin) 11:189–194, 1967

Hollister LE, Jones KP, Brownfield B, et al: Chlorpromazine alone and with reserpine: use in the treatment of mental disease. California Medicine 83:218–221, 1955

Kandel ER, Schwartz JH: Principles of Neural Science, 2nd Edition. New York, Elsevier, 1985, p 711

King DJ: Dopamine agonists for negative symptoms in schizophrenia. Br J Clin Pharmacol 6:541–542, 1978

Kinross-Wright V: Chlorpromazine and reserpine in the treatment of psychoses. Ann NY Acad Sci 61:174–182, 1955

Larsson M, Ohman R, Wallin L, et al: Antipsychotic treatment with alpha-methyltyrosine in combination with thioridazine: prolactin response and interaction with dopaminergic precursor pools. J Neural Transm 60:115–132, 1984

Lasky JJ, Klett CJ, Caffey EM, et al: Drug treatment of schizophrenic patients: a comparative evaluation of chlorpromazine, chlorprothixene, fluphenazine, reserpine, thioridazine, and triflupromazine. Diseases of the Nervous System 23:698–706, 1962

Levy MI, Davis BM, Mohs RC, et al: Gamma-hydroxybutyrate in the treatment of schizophrenia. Psychiatry Res 9:1–8, 1983

Magelund G, Gerlach J, Casey DE: Neuroleptic-potentiating effect of alpha-methyl-p-tyrosine compared with haloperidol and placebo in a double-blind cross-over trial. Acta Psychiatr Scand 60:185–189, 1979a

Magelund G, Gerlach J, Casey DE: Neuroleptic-potentiating effect of metyrosine (letter). Am J Psychiatry 136:732, 1979b

Meltzer HY, Kolakowska T, Robertson A, et al: Effect of low-dose bromocriptine in treatment of psychosis: the dopamine autoreceptor-stimulation strategy. Psychopharmacology 81:37–41, 1983

Nasrallah HA, Donnelly EF, Bigelow LB, et al: Inhibition of dopamine synthesis in chronic schizophrenia. Arch Gen Psychiatry 34:649–655, 1977

Schulz SC, Van Kammen DP, Buchsbaum MS, et al: Gamma-hydroxybutyrate treatment of schizophrenia: a pilot study. Pharmacopsychiatria 14:129–132, 1981

Tamminga CA: Antipsychotic and antidyskinetic properties of ergot dopamine agonists, in Ergot Compounds and Brain Function: Neuroendocrine and Neuropsychiatric Aspects. Edited by Goldstein M. New York, Raven, 1980

Tamminga CA, Schaffer MH: Treatment of schizophrenia with ergot derivatives. Psychopharmacology 66:239–242, 1979

Tanaka Z, Mukai A, Takayanagi Y, et al: Clinical application of 4-hydroxybutyrate sodium and 4-butyrolactone in neuropsychiatric patients. Folia Psychiatrica et Neurologica 20:9–17, 1966

Trabucchi M, Andreoli VM, Frattola L, et al: Pre- and postsynaptic action of bromocriptine: its pharmacological effects in schizophrenia and neurological diseases. Adv Biochem Psychopharmacol 16:661–665, 1977

Tuteur W, Lepson D: Combined reserpine-chlorpromazine therapy in highly disturbed psychotics, in Tranquilizing Drugs. Edited by Himwich HE. Washington, DC, American Association for the Advancement of Science, 1957, pp 163–172

Van Putten T, Mutalipessi CR, Malkin MD: Phenothiazine-induced decompensation. Arch Gen Psychiatry 30:102–105, 1974

Walinder J. Skott A, Carlsson A, et al: Potentiation by metyrosine of thioridazine effects in chronic schizophrenics. Arch Gen Psychiatry 33:501–505, 1976

Chapter 9

Clozapine in Refractory Schizophrenia

John M. Kane, M.D.
Jeffrey A. Lieberman, M.D.
Celeste A. Johns, M.D.

Chapter 9

Clozapine in Refractory Schizophrenia

Although the availability of neuroleptic (or antipsychotic) drugs has been a major benefit for the long-term treatment of schizophrenia, a variety of factors have limited the utility of the compounds. First, not all patients derive the same degree of benefit, with some patients improving little if at all after a full trial of treatment. Second, even among patients who do respond, the medications are not effective against the full range of symptomatology and deficits that these patients experience. Third, antipsychotic drugs are associated with a variety of adverse effects, particularly neurologic. Although the more acute extrapyramidal side effects (e.g., dystonia, akinesia, akathisia) may respond to dosage reduction or other pharmacologic treatments, many patients experience these effects as distressing or uncomfortable and they may frequently go undetected by clinicians. In effect, these reactions may contribute in important ways to the development of noncompliance in medication taking, a chronic problem in the long-term treatment of schizophrenia. In addition, these adverse effects can mimic anxiety, agitation, or even so-called negative symptoms (emotional withdrawal, blunted affect, psychomotor retardation). The longer-term adverse effects, such as tardive dyskinesia and tardive dystonia, may be much more serious in that a proportion of cases are persistent, severe, and potentially disabling.

It is not surprising, therefore, that continued efforts have been directed toward the development of new compounds that might offer some advantages in therapeutic efficacy or reduced propensity for specific adverse effects. At the same time, research has been underway to understand the etiology and pathophysiology of schizophrenia in ways that might lead to improved treatment approaches. A sober review of these areas, however, shows few if any gains in terms of real advances in drug development or our understanding of why some patients benefit substantially from available medication and others benefit hardly at all. (This does not in any way negate the importance of those substantial advances that have been made in our ability to use available treatments most appropriately and effectively, because this too has enormous public health implications.)

CLINICAL TRIALS

Numerous clinical trials have been conducted comparing one neuroleptic to another; however, there has been no compelling evidence that any one drug or one drug class is more effective than another (Davis et al. 1980; Klein and Davis 1969). Still clinicians continue to make anecdotal observations with very occasional research confirmation (Gardos 1978) that switching from one drug to another may be helpful in some patients who have failed to respond adequately. (This issue is discussed in more detail by Johns et al. [Chapter 4, this volume].)

After patients have had multiple courses of antipsychotic treatment and continue to remain very symptomatic, we have few alternatives to offer. Although numerous reports (most anecdotal, a few controlled) have suggested occasional benefit from various somatic or pharmacologic treatments (e.g., lithium, electroconvulsive therapy, propranolol), none of these treatments hold consistent promise for most treatment-resistant patients. Given developments in further identifying neuroanatomic and neuropathologic abnormalities in the brains of some schizophrenic patients, there has been the suggestion that perhaps we should not reasonably expect pharmacologic treatments to be useful in certain subtypes of the illness.

Against this background, the accumulating data base with clozapine (Clozaril) over the past several years has led to some renewed optimism regarding further advances in the pharmacologic treatment of schizophrenia.

CLOZAPINE

Clozapine belongs to the dibenzodiazepine class and is related chemically to the antipsychotic drug loxapine. However, its pharmacologic characteristics differ from those of loxapine. Clozapine has greater serotonergic (S_2), adrenergic (α_1), and histaminergic (H_1) blocking activity relative to its dopamine blocking effects and is also a potent muscarinic acetylcholine receptor antagonist (Peroutka and Snyder 1980; Richelson 1984). Compared to most classic neuroleptics, it has a lower affinity for D_2 receptors and binds proportionally more to D_1 receptors (Hyttel et al. 1985). In addition, it appears to act more selectively at cortical and limbic dopamine neuronal systems in preference to the nigrostriatal and tubero infundibular regions (Kane et al. 1981; Meltzer et al. 1979). The relationship between these characteristics and clozapine's novel clinical effects remain speculative.

Both initial preclinical and clinical research suggested that clozapine might have properties that were unusual for classic neuroleptics and might hold great promise for clinical application. These included potential therapeutic superiority over available antipsychotic agents and a substantially more favorable profile of extrapyramidal side effects, specifically, a reduced propensity to produce acute extrapyramidal side effects and possibly tardive dyskinesia.

Despite this initial potential, a series of cases of agranulocytosis that occurred in Finland in 1975 (de la Chapelle et al. 1977; Griffith and Saameli 1975) resulted in a temporary suspension of further development of the drug in both the United States and Europe. At the same time, however, with increased caution and surveillance of white blood cell counts, some patients were allowed to be treated with the drug on an ongoing basis for humanitarian purposes.

In the mid-1980s, it was clear that the literature provided evidence from a series of studies both in the United States and in Europe (Claghorn et al. 1987; Fischer-Cornelssen and Ferner 1976) that clearly established the antipsychotic efficacy of clozapine in schizophrenic patients. The apparent significantly higher incidence of agranulocytosis associated with this compound, however, created a dilemma with regard to the potential marketing of the drug in the United States and several other countries. At the same time, the results of trials previously conducted and clinical experience with the drug did suggest that some patients who had proven to be unresponsive to available antipsychotic agents might show important therapeutic gains with clozapine. As a result, the question arose as to whether or not the benefit-to-risk ratio involved with clozapine treatment might be acceptable for a population of carefully selected treatment-refractory patients.

In considering this issue, one should also keep in mind the enormous morbidity and even mortality associated with chronic, treatment-resistant schizophrenia. It is also important to note that the time course of agranulocytosis development in the majority of cases showed the period of maximum risk to be between the 6th and 18th week of clozapine treatment. As a result, it seemed feasible to design a trial that could identify those patients deriving clinically important benefits from clozapine before establishing the need to expose the patient to the maximum level of risk of agranulocytosis.

MULTICENTER TRIAL

With these various considerations, it was felt that a large, carefully designed multicenter trial focusing specifically on treatment-refractory patients would be necessary to establish clearly the superiority of clozapine in this context prior to its being approved for marketing.

The results of this study have been published (Kane et al. 1988). A total of 268 patients who met DSM-III (American Psychiatric Association 1980) criteria for schizophrenia and conservative criteria for previous refractoriness to treatment participated in a double-blind comparison of clozapine and chlorpromazine (plus benztropine). Sixteen institutions in the United States contributed patients to the protocol.

Methods

Patients were considered refractory to standard treatment if they met the following criteria: 1) had at least three periods of treatment in the preceding 5 years with neuroleptic agents (from at least two different chemical classes) at doses equivalent to 1,000 mg/day or higher of chlorpromazine for a period of 6 weeks, each without significant symptomatic relief; and 2) no period of good functioning within the preceding 5 years. In addition, subjects had to meet the following psychopathologic severity criteria: total Brief Psychiatric Rating Scale (BPRS) (Overall and Gorham 1962) score of at least 45, plus a minimum Clinical Global Impressions (CGI) rating of 4 (moderately ill). In addition, item scores of at least 4 (moderate) were required on two of the following four BPRS items: conceptual disorganization, suspiciousness, hallucinatory behavior, and unusual thought content.

All patients who met eligibility criteria and signed informed consent entered a prospective period of treatment with haloperidol (up to 60 mg/day or higher) plus benztropine (6 mg/day) for 6 weeks to confirm drug responsiveness. Improvement in this context was defined a priori as a 20% decrease on the BPRS total score plus either a posttreatment CGI rating of mildly ill (3 or less) or a posttreatment BPRS total score of 35 or less. Any patients who responded to haloperidol (i.e., meeting the improvement criteria as defined) were dropped from further study.

Those individuals who met the multiple symptom criteria and who failed to respond to the 6 weeks of haloperidol were then randomly assigned to a subsequent 6-week, double-blind trial of either clozapine up to 900 mg/day or chlorpromazine up to 1,800 mg/day plus benztropine 6 mg/day.

Prior to the start of the study, a priori criteria supportive to the superiority of clozapine in this patient population were agreed upon. These criteria required statistical superiority to be proven in *all* of the three following areas: 1) the CGI; 2) changes in the BPRS total score;

and 3) significant improvement in at least two of the following four BPRS items: conceptual disorganization, hallucinatory behavior, suspiciousness, and unusual thought content (or the cluster score derived from summing these four items).

The mean (± SD) age of the patients participating was 36 ± 8.9. Their duration of current symptoms averaged 314 weeks, and their age at first hospitalization 20.4 years. The median number of previous hospitalizations was 7, and the median length of the current hospitalization was 104 weeks.

Results

The mean peak dose of chlorpromazine employed in the study exceeded 1,200 mg/day, and the mean peak dose of clozapine exceeded 600 mg/day. The 6-week, double-blind study was completed by 88% of the clozapine-treated patients and 87% of the chlorpromazine-treated patients. Rates of early termination for all reasons were similar for patients in both treatment groups. The results of this study indicated that on both the BPRS total score and the CGI there was significantly greater improvement among the clozapine-treated patients. Differences favoring clozapine were statistically significant by the first week of treatment and continued to be present weekly over the entire course of the study. Similarly, the four BPRS psychotic items alluded to previously all demonstrated significant differences favoring clozapine. Clozapine also proved to be superior in the treatment of those items on the BPRS reflective of negative symptoms (i.e., emotional withdrawal, blunted affect, psychomotor retardation, and disorientation).

Patients were categorized as having "improved" to a significant extent or not over the course of the double-blind trial utilizing a priori criteria. These criteria included a reduction of at least 20% from baseline on the BPRS total score, plus either a posttreatment CGI scale score of 3 (mild) or less, or a posttreatment BPRS total score of 35 or lower. When these criteria were applied across all patients who completed at least 1 week of the double-blind phase of treatment, it was found that only 4% of the chlorpromazine patients had improved as compared to 30% of the clozapine patients ($P < .001$).

The two treatments did not differ in the proportion of patients who experienced a drop in total white blood cell count below 3,900: 4.9% for clozapine and 3.3% for chlorpromazine. Of the clozapine-treated patients, 13% experienced a drop in neutrophils to below 50% of the total white blood cell count in comparison to 20% of the patients on chlorpromazine. There were no reports of agranulocytosis in this cohort. Those cases of agranulocytosis that have occurred in the

United States have been among individuals treated in an open-label humanitarian protocol. The current estimates regarding the risk of agranulocytosis with clozapine continue to exceed those typically associated with other antipsychotic drugs (Lieberman et al. 1988). In the United States, by mid-1990, 18 patients had developed this problem, all of whom have recovered without any apparent long-term effect. Using a life-table method of calculating risk, data from the United States indicate a 2% cumulative incidence of agranulocytosis over 52 weeks of clozapine treatment.

Discussion

This controlled trial provided the first systematic data that any specific antipsychotic drug is superior to another in a carefully selected, well-defined group of treatment refractory patients who have proven unresponsive to haloperidol and other available neuroleptics. These results are very encouraging, not only in suggesting the possible utility of clozapine for some refractory patients, but also in supporting the possibility that some pharmacologic response may be possible even among severely ill, chronic, refractory patients.

An important question yet to be addressed pertains to the extent to which these gains can be sustained over longer intervals. It is undoubtedly unrealistic to expect the full consequences of any meaningful symptomatic improvement in a patient population such as this to be apparent during a 6-week trial. On the other hand, if these improvements can be sustained and patients become more responsive to a variety of other psychosocial and vocational treatment modalities, perhaps important steps can be achieved toward overcoming their various secondary disabilities.

ADDITIONAL STUDIES

Three long-term follow-up studies conducted in Scandinavia provide support for clozapine's ability to sustain the types of improvements that have been observed over many months or even years.

Juul Povlsen et al. (1985) reported on a retrospective investigation of 216 patients treated with clozapine for up to 12 years in Denmark. Of the 216, 85 were treated exclusively with clozapine; the remaining 131 received additional medication. Their mean age was 37 years, and the mean duration of psychosis was 13 years. The mean duration of clozapine treatment was 2.75 years. All of the 216 patients had been hospitalized and were treated with clozapine between 1971 and 1983. This patient population had previously been treated with one or more neuroleptics and either had failed to respond adequately or their response was limited by side effects. A global estimation of the therapeutic effects revealed that for one-third of the patients, clozapine, either alone or in combination with other neuroleptic drugs, was significantly better than previous antipsychotic therapy, although between 47% and 63% of the patients showed no appreciable change. The authors were unable to identify any clinical demographic or treatment history characteristics that were successful in predicting improvement on clozapine.

Kuha and Miettinen (1986) conducted a retrospective study of 108 chronic schizophrenic patients (55 men and 53 women) treated with clozapine for up to 7 years in Finland. Their mean age was 36 years, and all patients were suffering from chronic schizophrenia according to DSM-III criteria. The mean duration of illness was 15 years, the mean number of hospitalizations was 10 years, and the mean duration of cumulative hospitalization was 8 years. All of the patients had received a variety of neuroleptic agents 4 years prior to the initiation of clozapine. The mean duration of clozapine treatment was 1.5 years. Of the 108 patients studied, approximately one-third were noted to have experienced an extremely distinct effect following clozapine treatment, particularly improvement in hallucinations and delusions. These investigators suggested a relationship between length of prior treatment as inpatients and success following treatment with clozapine, with the shorter duration of inpatient hospitalization being associated with a better response to clozapine. This is an important lead to pursue; it may well be that, for those patients who have been refractory for a shorter duration than those in the United States multicenter study, the response might prove to be superior.

Lindstrom (1987) conducted a retrospective study in 96 patients (64 men and 32 women) treated with clozapine for up to 13 years in Sweden. Their mean age was 36 years at the time of follow-up. Their mean duration of illness at the time clozapine was initiated was 8.7 years, and the mean duration of subsequent clozapine treatment was 3.6 years. All patients had previously been treated with a variety of different neuroleptics. In 85%, the reason for initiating clozapine was insufficient clinical improvement with other compounds.

The global evaluation of clinical efficacy of clozapine revealed a significant improvement in 43% of the patients, and in 38% clozapine was judged to be "moderately" better than the previous neuroleptic treatment. Interestingly, the ability to maintain employment was assessed 2 years after clozapine treatment was initiated. Of the 62 patients who were on clozapine after 2 years, 39% were employed either as full-time or as half-time employees. Before clozapine treatment was initiated, only 3 of the 96 patients were employed.

The data on adverse effects with long-term treatment in these three follow-up studies suggest that fewer than 10% of patients discontinue clozapine because of untoward effects, and the risk of agranulocytosis was approximately 1% in these samples. In addition to agranulocytosis, clozapine does produce a variety of adverse effects that differ in type and frequency from those usually associated with available neuroleptics (Lieberman et al., in press). In the United States multicenter study described previously, the following adverse effects among clozapine-treated patients were reported: sedation 21%, tachycardia 17%, constipation 16%, dizziness 14%, hypotension 13%, hyperthermia 13%, and sialorrhea 13%. In addition, clozapine has been associated with grand mal seizures, and the frequency may be greater than that usually seen with neuroleptic drugs. Seizure risk with clozapine appears to be dose related. Based on data from United States cases, the frequency of seizures in patients treated with 600 mg/day or more was 14%; among patients treated with 300–600 mg/day, 1.8%; and for those treated with less than 300 mg/day, 0.6%.

CONCLUSIONS

Which patients should receive clozapine? At present, it would appear that those individuals suffering from a serious psychotic illness who are unresponsive to or cannot tolerate available antipsychotic agents are the appropriate candidates for a possible trial of clozapine. There are no clear-cut, well-validated criteria for defining treatment refractoriness. The criteria applied in the Kane et al. (1988) study did succeed in identifying a group of patients who failed to respond to trials of haloperidol and chlorpromazine, yet 30% did benefit from clozapine. We should emphasize that these patients were severely symptomatic (with a mean BPRS total score of 61 at baseline). It may be that these criteria are too stringent and further research should explore the full range of indications that may be appropriate for this compound. At present, clinical judgment will be necessary to determine the relative benefit-to-risk ratio in each individual case. It is necessary to acknowledge that the majority of refractory patients may not benefit substantially, but for the one-third who do, the compound may offer new hope. It is also apparent that in many cases improvement continues beyond the first 6-week trial and for patients who have been chronically ill and treatment refractory, it is likely that the addition of a variety of other treatment modalities following some symptomatic improvement could provide further gains in overcoming psychosocial and vocational disabilities.

Patients who are intolerant of traditional neuroleptics may also be appropriate candidates for clozapine treatment, particularly patients who experience clinically significant extrapyramidal side effects, such as tardive dyskinesia or tardive dystonia. This is not an indication that is included in the package labeling; therefore, all the cautions that should be employed in using a medication in that context would apply. There is evidence that does suggest that clozapine has a reduced or absent propensity to produce persistent abnormal involuntary movements; therefore, its potential use as a treatment for individuals who have developed these adverse effects may be appropriate. It is hoped that considerable further research will provide additional guidance to the clinician with regard to indications, contraindications, and hopefully even predictors of response.

Patients and their families must be involved in the decision to use clozapine. The risks and benefits as well as the nature of the drug and the extensive monitoring required must be clearly explained. Documentation of this process should also be made in the medical record.

The use of this medication does provide some specific challenges and concerns, but it is a treatment that should be available to appropriate patients. As with any new medication, clinicians should familiarize themselves with its various properties prior to using it.

REFERENCES

American Psychiatric Association: Diagnostic and Statistical Manual of Mental Disorders, 3rd Edition. Washington, DC, American Psychiatric Association, 1980

Claghorn J, Honigfeld G, Abuzzahab FS, et al: The risks and benefits of clozapine versus chlorpromazine. J Clin Psychopharmacol 7:377–384, 1987

Davis JM, Schaffer CB, Killian GA, et al: Important issues in the drug treatment of schizophrenia. Schizophr Bull 6:70–87, 1980

De la Chapelle A, Kari C, Nurminen M, et al: Clozapine-induced agranulocytosis. Hum Genet 37:183–194, 1977

Fischer-Cornelssen KA, Ferner UJ: An example of European multicenter trials: multispectral analysis of clozapine. Psychopharmacol Bull 12:34–39, 1976

Gardos G: Are antipsychotic drugs interchangeable? J Nerv Ment Dis 159:343–348, 1978

Griffith RW, Saameli K: Clozapine and agranulocytosis. Lancet 2:657, 1975

Hyttel J, Larsen JJ, Christensen AV, et al: Receptor-binding profiles of neuroleptics, in Dyskinesia: Research and Treatment. Edited by Casey DE. New York, Springer-Verlag, 1985, pp 9–18

Juul Povlsen U, Noring U, Fog R, et al: Tolerability and therapeutic effect of clozapine: a retrospective investigation of 216 patients treated with clozapine for up to 12 years. Acta Psychiatr Scand 71:176–185, 1985

Kane JM, Cooper TB, Sachar EJ, et al: Clozapine: plasma levels and prolactin response. Psychopharmacology 73:184–187, 1981

Kane J, Honigfeld G, Singer J, et al: Clozapine for the treatment-resistant schizophrenic: a double-blind comparison with chlorpromazine. Arch Gen Psychiatry 45:789–796, 1988

Klein DF, Davis JM: Diagnosis and Drug Treatment of Psychiatric Disorders. Baltimore, MD, Williams & Wilkins, 1969

Kuha S, Miettinen E: Long term effect of clozapine in schizophrenia: a retrospective study of 108 chronic schizophrenics treated with clozapine for up to seven years. Nordisk Psykiatr Tidsfkr 40:225–230, 1986

Lieberman JA, Johns CA, Kane JM, et al: Clozapine induced agranulocytosis: non-cross reactivity with other psychotropic drugs. J Clin Psychiatry 49:271–277, 1988

Lieberman J, Kane J, Johns C: Clozapine: guidelines for clinical management. J Clin Psychiatry (in press)

Lindstrom LH: The effect of long-term treatment with clozapine in schizophrenia: a retrospective study in 96 patients treated with clozapine for up to 13 years. Acta Psychiatr Scand 945:1–6, 1987

Meltzer HY, Goode DJ, Schyve PM, et al: Effect of clozapine on human serum prolactin levels. Am J Psychiatry 136:1550–1555, 1979

Overall JE, Gorham DR: The Brief Psychiatric Rating Scale. Psychol Rep 10:799–812, 1962

Peroutka SJ, Snyder SH: Relationship of neuroleptic drug effects at brain dopamine, serotonin, adrenergic, and histamine receptors to clinical potency. Am J Psychiatry 137:1518–1522, 1980

Richelson E: Neuroleptic affinities for human brain receptors and their use in predicting adverse effects. J Clin Psychiatry 45:331–336, 1984